Thomas O. Summers

Dublin

An Historical Sketch of Ireland's Metropolis

Thomas O. Summers

Dublin
An Historical Sketch of Ireland's Metropolis

ISBN/EAN: 9783743420892

Manufactured in Europe, USA, Canada, Australia, Japa

Cover: Foto ©ninafisch / pixelio.de

Manufactured and distributed by brebook publishing software (www.brebook.com)

Thomas O. Summers

Dublin

AN HISTORICAL SKETCH

OF

IRELAND'S METROPOLIS.

EDITED BY THOMAS O. SUMMERS, D.D.

Nashville, Tenn.:
SOUTHERN METHODIST PUBLISHING HOUSE.
1860.

STEREOTYPED AND PRINTED BY A. A. STITT,
SOUTHERN METHODIST PUBLISHING HOUSE, NASHVILLE, TENN.

Preface.

It is proposed to give in this small volume, some account of a city which rules and graces one of the finest bays of the ocean—the metropolis of a country fraught with industrial resources beyond what most others possess, and peopled by a race proverbial for intelligence and hospitality, and certainly not inferior to their neighbors in many qualities necessary to form a prosperous and influential community.

Contents.

	Page
PREFACE	V

SECTION I.
DUBLIN PREVIOUS TO THE ELEVENTH CENTURY...... 7

SECTION II.
DUBLIN SUBJECT TO THE ENGLISH PAPAL RULE.... 29

SECTION III.
DUBLIN DURING THE BRITISH REFORMATION......... 60

SECTION IV.
DUBLIN UNDER JAMES I. AND CHARLES I............. 89

SECTION V.
DUBLIN AT THE COMMONWEALTH, THE RESTORATION, AND THE REVOLUTION........................... 111

SECTION VI.
DUBLIN IN THE EIGHTEENTH CENTURY................ 135

SECTION VII.
DUBLIN SINCE THE UNION WITH GREAT BRITAIN TO THE YEAR EIGHTEEN HUNDRED AND FIFTY........ 168

DUBLIN.

SECTION I.

DUBLIN PREVIOUS TO THE ELEVENTH CENTURY.

The earliest authentic notice of Dublin occurs in the geography of Ptolemy, who flourished in the second century of our era. His description of the world as then known begins with Hibernia, an honor which the country received from him because of its being the most western in Europe. His map of Ireland is much more correct in its outline than the one he has furnished of Great Britain: in the latter, the portion now called Scotland is made to bend off eastward, nearly at a right angle from the southern portion. He marks "Eblana" just where Dublin at present stands, and he describes it as "$\pi\acute{o}\lambda\iota\varsigma$," a *city*. The people inhabiting the range northward as far as the river Boyne, including part of Meath, he calls "Eblani," probably as belonging or subject to "Eblana," though some conjecture that the place took its name from the people, not the people theirs from the place.

That the words "Dublin" and "Eblana" were

at first one, is obvious. Indeed, it has been more than supposed that a letter has been lost from the original, and that Ptolemy wrote "*D*eblana." "Dublin" is composed of two Irish words,— "Dubh," *black*, and "Linn," *water*—the river which here empties itself into the sea being of a dark color, from its flowing over a bog.

The city was otherwise called "Ath-Cliath," the "Hurdle-Ford," and "Bally Ath-Cliath," the "Town of the Hurdle-Ford." Both names indicate that a passage was here made or marked by "hurdles" across the stream. Tradition reports that it was constructed for more safely conveying sheep from one side to the other; but whether it had at all the form of a "suspension-bridge" the account does not explain.

A fourth name given to the city in olden time, was "Droom-Choll-Coil," the "Brow of a Hazel-Wood," from its occupying the upper front of a rise of ground, other parts of which were covered with a wood of the kind mentioned.

Dublin must have been in Ptolemy's day, by report at least, a place of some size and importance, or he would not have styled it a "city." We should, however, greatly mistake if we conceived it to have been then an aggregation of houses, streets, and public buildings, such as the word suggests to us now. "The ancient Irish were at no trouble in providing for themselves habitations of solid and lasting materials. Their houses were built of twigs and hurdles, and covered with sedge or straw." Buildings of stone and mortar are believed to have been unknown in Ireland before the sixth century. For the introduction of what we call "architecture," the country is indebted to Christianity. The population of "Eblana" were unacquainted with our often costly and trouble-causing superfluities of boarded floors, glazed windows, paved ways, gas-lights, scavengering, sewerage, and police—matters which we moderns are apt to reckon among the necessaries of life. Let the reader, for a moment, in his conception sweep away the present "Dublin;" then group, without much regard to order, a few hundred "cabins," some of them larger than the rest, along the upper part of the range fronting the Liffey, from Cork Hill to Bridge street; next, clothe the top and southern descent of the ridge with a hazel-wood, which he may also carry round the eastern and western sides of the "city," and along between it and the river; finally, let him place a "hurdle-ford" where Whitworth Bridge now stands; and he will perhaps have as correct an idea of Ptolemy's "Eblana" as a model by Brunetti could supply.

Three orders of royalty then existed in Ireland. The country had its unity, its divisions, and its subdivisions of sovereignty. It was parcelled out under a large number of toparchs, or petty chiefs, each of whom bore the title of "king," as was the case in the early times of Palestine and its neighbor lands. Above these were five provincial monarchs, "kings" of a higher grade. One of the five reigned over all, as "king of Ireland:" his palace was on the hill of Tarah, in Meath, where he triennially convened the states of his realm, for enacting laws and other national business, and where he entertained his dignitaries with hospitality and magnificence worthy of his supremacy. "Eblana" had its "king," one of the lowest order of *royal* personages.

The food of the common people of ancient Ireland is said to have been "very mean and slender — namely, milk, butter, and herbs: from whence," writes Ware, "the Epitome of Strabo calls the Irish herb-eaters." The gentry and nobility lived in higher style. Had we entered a banqueting-hall of the Eblani on a great festival day, we might have found the company reclining on couches of grass or rushes, round a table furnished with griddle-baked bread, milk-meats, and varieties of fish and flesh, both boiled and roast. The cup, too, made of wood, or horn, or brass, filled with beer or mead — "whisky" was then unknown — was passed joyfully from guest to guest, while the metal-strung harp, obedient to the touch of skill and taste, sent forth stirring sounds, with which oft mingled those of the martial drum, accompanying the bard's recital of warm affection, of illustrious ancestry, and of heroic deeds.

Of trade and commerce Eblana had not much to boast: none of its people ranked as "merchant princes." Its Liffey was not crowded with shipping which brought in the produce of other lands, or bore away the growth and manufacture of its own. The risk incurred in crossing the bar from the sea, except at certain times of the tide, together with the scanty demands for articles of which there was not a home supply, made the arrival of a foreign vessel an "event" as great as was the visit of a European or American ship at Hawaii or Tahiti fifty years ago. The Eblani had pasturage for cattle and sheep. They were also engaged in agriculture, though of a somewhat humble order—the Irish plough being, centuries later, a small wooden instrument tied to the tail of an ox or a "hobby." Fishing was common. Their boats were of two kinds : one, a canoe formed out of the trunk of a tree, and called a "Cotti," of which a specimen is to be seen in the Royal Dublin Society's Museum. The other, called a "Corragh," consisted of a frame of wicker-work covered with hides, larger, longer, and otherwise more adapted for sea-work, but in materials and structure like the "corracles" still used on rivers in Wales and adjoining parts. It was in a "corragh" that Columba with his twelve companions went from Ireland to Iona, in the sixth century.

Learning and refinement among the Eblani can be judged of only from what is known of the Irish in general of those times, and even that information is scanty and precarious. The Ogham inscriptions are of a very high antiquity. We are told of schools at Tarah, where youths were trained for sacred and civic duties. The Irish warriors were "sworn to be the protectors of the fair, and avengers of their wrongs; and to be polite in word and address to their greatest enemies." "A character without guile or deceit was esteemed the highest that could be given among the ancient

Irish, and the favorite panegyric of a bard to his hero would be that he had a heart incapable of guile." The Irish were early acquainted with the game of chess. Their harp and song, too, have attained a world-wide fame. The former is believed to have been kept "sacredly unaltered" from the ages we are speaking of down to comparatively modern date, when Drayton wrote:—

> "The Irish I admire,
> And still cleave to that lyre
> As our muse's mother,
> And think, till I expire,
> Apollo's such another."

Bacon pronounced, "No harp hath the sound so melting and prolonged as the Irish harp;" and Evelyn wrote: "Such music before or since did I never hear—that instrument being neglected for its extraordinary difficulty; but in my judgment being far superior to the lute itself, or whatever speaks with strings." Ancient Erin was the home of poetic genius. Feargus, called "Fionbell, or the Sweet-voiced," was one of its most distinguished bards. An ode of his composition, delivered extempore, is said to have succeeded in blending in peace and friendship two chiefs, "Gaul the Son of Morni," and "Finn of the flowing locks," who, with their respective followers, had met on a field of strife to contend for spoils they had jointly won from a common foe. The following lines, from a translation of his "War Ode" to Osgar, the son of Ossian, at the battle of Gaura, when leading on his troops against Cairbre, the monarch of Ireland, towards the close of the third century, present a thought truly sublime :—

"Thine be the battle, thine the sway!
On, on to Cairbre hew thy conquering way,
And let thy deathful arm dash safety from his side!
  As the proud wave, on whose broad back
    The storm its burden heaves,
    Drives on the scattered wreck
      Its ruin leaves :
  So let thy sweeping progress roll,
    Fierce, resistless, rapid, strong—
Pour, like the billow of the flood, o'erwhelming might along."

The Cromlechs in the neighborhood of Dublin —one near the Hill of Howth, another on the south of Killiney Hill, and another at Cabinteely, about a mile westward—show that Druidism was the religion of the Eblani, as it was of other parts of the country. In due form and solemnity their priests ministered at the altar within the circle of stones, presenting, on behalf of the congregation outside the sacred enclosure, sacrifices and other homages to their Baalim, the sun, the moon, and the host of heaven. Holocausts of human beings were among the rites prescribed by that superstition. Fire was an object of worship, perhaps by tradition from the Shechinah. Mountains and trees, also, are said to have had divine honors paid to them. Groves of the oak were not wanting to aid devotion, and afford growth to the mistletoe. Then, as now, the faith of the people hung pieces of cloth on branches near a "holy well," to imbibe from the presence there a virtue which might be carried away and applied for the removal of disease, or for some other useful purpose. Moreover, the invisible, but, when angered, desolating Wind, was held in awe and propitiated, lest, neglected, it should break forth in fury and spread havoc around. It was a prevailing opinion that the Round Towers, of which there is one at Clondalkin, about three miles west of Dublin, and another at Swords, six miles north of the city, were Fire-temples. But Dr. Petrie seems to have exhausted the argument upon the subject, and concludes that they are buildings connected with Christianity.

It is certain that the gospel had found its way into Ireland previously to the fifth century, in the early part of which, as Prosper's Chronicle records, Palladius was sent by Celestine, bishop of Rome, "to the Scots believing in Christ," Ireland being then called "Scotia," and its inhabitants "Scoti," or Scots. How, when, or by whom the Christian faith first came into the country, we know not, but the honor of converting the Irish nation is commonly ascribed to St. Patrick, who came to evangelize them, shortly after the mission and death of Palladius. Sir William Betham, however, than whom few antiquaries have given more attention to the question, thinks that the true Patrick, whose labors so eminently contributed to Christianize the people, lived and did his work long before Palladius existed. Without entering upon that inquiry, we may notice the account which a tradition gives of the gospel being brought to Dublin. It is, that

Patrick, having preached with great success in Ulster and Connaught, came into Meath and Leinster, and took Dublin on his way southward: that having crossed the Finglass river to the rising ground within a mile of the city, perhaps near the site of Phibbsborough, he pronounced upon it a prophetic benediction, affirming that the city "should increase in riches and dignities, until at length it should be lifted up unto the throne of the kingdom:" that when he reached Dublin he preached to the king, Alphin Mac Eochaid, and his subjects, who received the divine message, and were baptized at a well, south of the city; and that the saint founded a church near this well, where now stands St. Patrick's cathedral. This is said to have occurred in the year 448. The detail is not vouched for by high authority, but it is the only one that tradition has preserved.

We have good evidence that the religion taught by Patrick, properly so called, was not that decreed by the Council of Trent, professed in the creed of Pope Pius IV., and disseminated by the propagandas of Rome and Lyons. In other words, it much more resembled New Testament Christianity than modern Romanism. Patrick found a number of churches and bishops in Ireland. He himself formed three hundred and sixty-five churches, and ordained over them an equal number of bishops, and three thousand presbyters; but he subjected none of them to the Roman see. The worship of the Virgin, transubstantiation, the adoration of images, restricting the reading of the Sacred Scriptures, and many other things now insisted upon as parts of the gospel, were not then recognized even by the Church at Rome. In the transactions of the Royal Irish Academy is published a translation, by Dr. Petrie, of a hymn composed by St. Patrick when he was about to visit Temur, or Tarah, and preach the gospel to Leogaire, the monarch of all Ireland. The visit was critical to Patrick himself, and to the cause he was embarked in. The adherents of the old paganism were prepared to withstand, as best they could, the assault he was about to make upon it in its highest places. Though it be not connected with Dublin in particular, yet, as throwing light on the doctrine which Patrick taught there, this " Hymn" will be interesting to the reader, and he shall have the translation of it before him entire:

"At Temur," [that is, Tarah, the court of the king,] "to-day I invoke the mighty power of the Trinity. I believe in the Trinity under the God of the elements.

"At Temur to-day (I place) the virtue of the birth of Christ with his baptism, the virtue of his crucifixion with his burial, the virtue of his resurrection with his ascension, the virtue of his coming to the eternal judgment.

"At Temur to-day (I place) the virtue of the love of Seraphim, (the virtue which exists) in the obedience of angels, in the hope of the resurrection to eternal reward, in the prayers of the noble fathers, in the predictions of the prophets, in the preaching of the apostles, in the faith of the confession, in the purity of the holy virgins, in the deeds of just men.

"At Temur to-day (I place) the strength of heaven, the light of the sun, the rapidity of lightning, the swiftness of the wind, the depth of the sea, the stability of the earth, the hardness of rocks (between me and the powers of paganism and demons.)

"At Temur to-day may the strength of God pilot me, may the power of God preserve me, may the wisdom of God instruct me, may the eye of God view me, may the ear of God hear me, may the word of God render me eloquent, may the hand of God protect me, may the mercy of God direct me, may the shield of God defend me, may the host of God guard me, against the snares of demons, the temptations of vices, the inclinations of the mind, against every man who meditates evil to me, far or near, alone or in company.

"I place all these powers between me and every evil unmerciful power directed against my body, (as a protection) against the incantations of false prophets; against the black laws of gentilism; against the false laws of heresy; against the treachery of idolatry; against the spells of women, snaiths, and Druids; against every knowledge which binds the soul of man. May Christ to-day protect me against poison, against burning, against drowning, against wounding, until I deserve much reward.

"Christ be with me, Christ before me, Christ after me, Christ in me, Christ under me, Christ over me, Christ at my right, Christ at my left,

Christ at this side, Christ at that side, Christ at my back.

"Christ be in the heart of each person whom I speak to; Christ in the mouth of each person who speaks to me; Christ in each eye that sees me; Christ in each ear which hears me.

"At Temur to-day I invoke the almighty power of the Trinity. I believe in the Trinity under the unity of the God of the elements.

"Salvation is the Lord's, salvation is the Lord's, salvation is Christ's. May thy salvation, O Lord, be always with me."

The above document, of the genuineness of which no doubt appears to exist, may not present the trust of Christian piety in the clear and strong light of New Testament instruction. It corresponds rather with the mysticism which had begun to creep over the Church about the time of Jerome. But it shows a heart that looked for help to Christ alone as God our Saviour. It gives no token of the "ever Blessed and Immaculate Virgin," the "never-failing Star of Hope," the "Help of Christians," the "Most Holy Mother," being "constantly and fervently invoked," "as the general patroness of all Ireland," as the synod at Thurles, in the year 1850, prescribed she should be; although, if at any time that zealous and devout man, St. Patrick, had judged it right and useful to seek her aid, he surely would have implored it under the circumstances which led him to compose the "Hymn" given above.

The notices which we have of Dublin previous

THE ELEVENTH CENTURY. 19

to the arrival of the Danes, an event which is believed to have occurred towards the close of the fifth century, are extremely meagre and uncertain. Almost the only item of information beyond what has been stated, is that about the beginning of the third century a division was made of the country into two portions, by a line running direct across it from Dublin on the east coast to Galway on the west. The northern portion or kingdom was called *Leath Quinn*, or the Half of *Quinn* or *Conn*, and the southern was called *Leath Mogha*, or the Half of *Eoghan*, or *Mogha*, king of Munster. The termination of the separation line eastward is said to have been where High street now stands.

The Danes were usually called "Ostmen," or *men from the east*, in Ireland, as in England and France they were called "Northmen," or Normans, *men from the north*—the name being given in each case according to the relative position of the country whence they came. It is not unlikely that their first landing at Dublin was for trade rather than for war or plunder. The place of their settlement was styled "Ostmantown," now changed into "Oxmantown," a district on the north side of the Liffey, at present partly occupied by the Royal Barracks, and perhaps nearly answering to Arran Quay Ward in the municipal divisions of the city. Some respectable authorities maintain that the Danes were unknown in Ireland till near the middle of the ninth century.

Dr. Lanigan, in his Ecclesiastical History of Ireland, not only rejects the story of the inhabitants of Dublin and their king having been converted by the preaching of St. Patrick, but states that the city had no bishop till the eleventh century. In the latter particular he is in error, unless by a " bishop" he intends a prelate of the Romish Church. The name of seven persons who were bishops of Dublin during the seventh and eighth centuries are given by Ware. There were also monastic establishments formed at Kilmainham, Clondalkin, Tallaght, and a few other places in the vicinity. In those times, Ireland was eminent for her schools of learning, and for the piety and zeal of her monks. About the year 564, St. Columba and twelve companions left the country and settled in Iona.* Other monks from Ireland located themselves and labored with much zeal in the north of England. Many others, again, passed over to the continent, and devoted themselves to Christianize and civilize its then barbarous population, until the power of Rome's bishop obliged them to conform or flee. What proportion, or whether any, of these earnest men went from Dublin or its neighborhood is unknown.

The venerable Bede records that, in the seventh century, numbers of the nobility and others of England went over to Ireland, on account of the advantages it afforded above their own country for education and religious improvement. Among the persons of high rank who thus made it a temporary residence, was Alfrid, a

---

* For information on this point, the reader is referred to Dr. Alexander's volume on Iona, in our catalogue.

son of Oswin, the king of Northumberland. Oswin, urged by the agents of Rome to recognize her rule, held an assembly for discussing in his presence the difference of opinion between them and the Irish monks—who till then had ministered to his people—respecting the observance of Easter. The design of the conference was to supply argument which would enable the king to form a sound judgment for his own guidance. In the end, Oswin, to make himself sure of the favor of Peter, who was represented as holding the keys of heaven, gave his verdict in favor of the Roman clergy, and the Irish monks were obliged forthwith to leave Northumbria and return to their native land. On the death of Oswin, his son Egfrid succeeded him in the throne, and Alfrid, his other son, withdrew to Ireland, dreading his brother's jealousy. In June, 684, Egfrid sent an expedition, under a commander named Beret, against the district called Bergia, lying between Dublin and Drogheda. The marauders spared neither laity nor clergy, things sacred nor things secular, and bore away with them "many captives and much booty." It is possible that the favorable treatment given to Alfrid may have provoked this outrage. Alfrid is said to have become, while in Ireland, "a man most learned in the Scriptures," and "highly qualified for being placed at the head of a state," which position he acquired when his brother died. A poem, composed by Alfrid, is yet extant in the Irish language, describing, in a lively strain, what he had observed in travelling through various parts of the country. It is too long to be inserted entire, but three stanzas may be transcribed as given in a translation:

> "I found the good lay monks and brothers
> Ever beseeching help for others,
> And, in their keeping, the holy word
> Pure as it came from Jesus the Lord.
>
> "I found in Leinster the smooth and sleek,
> From Dublin to Slewmargy's peak,
> Flourishing pastures, valor, health,
> Long-living worthies, commerce, wealth.
>
> "I found in Meath's fair principality,
> Virtue, vigor, and hospitality,
> Candor, joyfulness, bravery, purity—
> Ireland's bulwark and security."

With regard to what is said of the Irish monks "ever beseeching help for others," the reader will observe that it was for *others*, not for *themselves*, that they sought assistance; and it ought to be borne in mind that the Irish monks had it as a law that they were not to live upon alms, but were to support themselves by their own industry. The mention of "commerce" in Leinster naturally refers to Dublin, that city being, it is presumed, the principal, if not then the only seaport in the province. Slewmargy is a mountain in the Queen's County. In the third of the above stanzas, there are allusions to Tarah, where the monarch of all Ireland held his court.

Supposing the Danes to have settled in or near Dublin, as before noticed, towards the close of the fifth century, they must have lived on good terms with its native inhabitants, for we have no accounts of disagreements between the two parties till about the year 838. By that time, however, they appear to have become masters of the place, and their power had so increased that it aroused the fears of the local Irish chiefs around. In 851, the kings of Leinster and Meath made war upon them, expelled them from the city, and gave it up to pillage by a rude soldiery. But, in the year following, the Danes returned in great power, regained the place, fortified it with a wall and towers, and crowned their leader, Amlaffe, "king" of Dublin. He built himself a royal residence at Clondalkin. Hostilities frequently occurred between him and the neighboring princes. On one occasion they attacked Clondalkin, burned his palace there, and slew a hundred of his servants. He retaliated, by surprising a body of their followers, two thousand in number, all of whom he either killed or made prisoners. He made excursions into the country, and, among other successful enterprises, he plundered and burned Armagh. In 870, he and his son Yvar crossed the channel with an army to assist their brethren, the Danes, against the Saxons in England. The Ulster Annals relate their return thus: "Amlaffe and Yvar came to Ath-Cliath, out of Albany, with two hundred ships, and brought with them a great prey of English, Britons, and Picts." In 872, Ostin Mac Amlaffe, king of Dublin, invaded the Picts of North Britain with success, but was afterwards slain by his own people. On the other hand, in 890,

Dublin was taken by Gregory, king of Scotland. Two years afterwards, a great fleet of Danes arrived in the Liffey, to assist their countrymen, but on disembarking they were routed near the city with great slaughter. In 916, the Danes sustained the greatest defeat they ever had experienced in the country; yet, strange to record, in that same year they ravaged the island of Anglesea; and in three years more they vanquished and slew Neill IV., king of Ireland, in a battle near their city.

The long recital of constantly occurring fights, maraudings, and bloodshed, at which the preceding paragraph merely affords a glance, is interrupted by a statement that, about the year 948, the Danes of Dublin renounced heathenism and embraced Christianity. As will appear in our next section, it was Christianity as then Romanized, not Christianity as it existed among the native Irish, that they received. This circumstance will account for the outrages the Danes of Dublin continued to practice on their Irish neighbors, so strongly complained of by Dr. Lanigan, the ecclesiastical historian of Ireland: "These new converts," he writes, "did not imbibe the meekness prescribed by the gospel; for in 950," only two years after their conversion, "the Danes of Dublin plundered and burned Slane; so that many persons assembled in the belfry perished in the flames." About the time they became nominally Christians, they founded the Abbey of St. Mary, near Ostmantown, their own settlement. As the best sites were chosen for such establishments, we may presume that the portion of the city now traversed by Capel street, and its branches right and left, was then a spot the most eligible, for its rich soil, lovely position, and other conveniences, that the Danes had at their command in the neighborhood of Dublin.

Rapin informs us that Edgar, surnamed the Peaceable, king of England, kept a fleet of four thousand vessels, by which he not only protected his own dominions, but "obliged the kings of Wales, Ireland, and the Isle of Man, to swear allegiance to him, and acknowledge him for sovereign." This account of the extent of Edgar's rule corresponds with statements in a charter granted by him at Gloucester, 964. In that document he claims to have subdued under his power, "by the propitious grace of God," "together with the empire of the English, all the kingdoms of the islands of the ocean, with their fierce kings, as far as Norway, and the greatest part of Ireland, with its most noble city, Dublin." It is probable that the "king of Ireland," mentioned in Rapin, is the Danish king of Dublin, who was also sovereign of all the Danes in other parts of the country, including Limerick and Waterford. How long the king of Dublin remained subject to the king of England is not reported; but coins exist, which were struck at "Dyfelin," or Dublin, bearing the name of Ethelred, who was next but one in succession to Edgar on the English throne. Consequently there was a "mint" in the city, in the latter half of the tenth century.

The year 980 saw the Danes of Dublin routed by Malachi, king of Ireland, in an engagement at Tarah; and nine years afterwards, the same Malachi assailed them in their own quarters in Dublin, slew great numbers of them, remained there three-score nights, and pressed them so close in their camp on the shore outside the city, that they had no drink but the salt water. At length they submitted, and agreed to pay an ounce of gold out of every messuage and garden in Dublin, to him and his successors, yearly at Christmas.

While these matters were transpiring, another person was rising in power, who made his name one of the most famed in ancient Irish history. This was Brien Boroomh, king of Munster, who ere long became king of the whole country. In the year 999, the Dublin Danes ravaged a great part of Leinster, and brought back, among other prisoners, the king of the province, who was one of Brien's liegeman. Brien, on hearing this, marched with a select body of troops to Dublin, delivered the king of Leinster, banished the Danish king Sitricus beyond the seas, burned a great part of the city, and brought away a considerable quantity of gold and silver, with manufactured goods and other valuable effects. The citizens gave hostages, and were allowed to repair their works. Brien continued to pursue his conquests and depredations in other parts of Ireland. In 1013, however, the king of Leinster and the Danes of Dublin joined in a league against him. He laid the province waste to the very walls of the city, and, early in the following year, engaged many of the Irish princes to unite with him in a grand effort either to destroy the Danes, or compel them to quit the country altogether. Their monarch, Sitricus, with the Leinster king, were not slow in making preparations to defeat him. Aids came from the Isle of Man and the Hebrides. On Good Friday, April 23d, 1014, the hostile armies met on the plains of Clontarf, each resolved on victory or death. The place has thence been called the Marathon of Ireland. Both armies were in three divisions. The Danes had a thousand men in complete armor, and nine thousand Leinster troops, with their auxiliaries. A portion of Brien's followers were absent. The king of Meath, with a thousand soldiers, came obedient to Brien's call; but had a private understanding with the king of Leinster, that he and his troops would desert Brien in the hour of battle. The conflict was tremendous—the carnage fearful. It began at sunrise, and till four in the afternoon the issue remained doubtful. The Irish battle-axe, wielded with one hand, cleft in twain the armed Dane at a single stroke; but prodigies of valor were performed by all the combatants, and on both sides the victors of one moment fell victims the next. According to some accounts, Brien's forces gained the day: according to others, the Danes at first gave way, but rallied, and at last prevailed. Brien, it is said, when he had harangued his forces in the early morning, and the signal for battle was given, was not allowed by his followers to head them in the strife, on account of his great age, (eighty-three years,) but retired to his tent, where he was attacked, at the close of the engagement, by a party of Danes, and slain. On his side fell, also, his son, a long catalogue of princely and noble leaders, together with from seven to eleven thousand men. On the other side fell the king of Leinster, almost all his princes and chiefs, and three thousand men: while the Danes lost their principal officers and fourteen thousand men, including the thousand in coats of mail, who, it is said, were all cut to pieces. After the battle, Sitricus, with the Irish Danes, returned to Dublin, and those from foreign parts went on board their vessels, and set sail homewards. Some report that Brien's body and his son's were interred at Kilmainham, "a village about a mile from Dublin, near an old stone cross;" but it is believed by others that his corpse was conveyed to Swords, and then removed, pursuant to his own directions, and buried in Armagh.

Brien Boroomh is renowned for his superiority in statesmanship and in music, equally as in war. What is said to have been *his* harp is preserved in the museum of the Dublin University; but its identity is apocryphal, and were it proved that the instrument was Brien's, a deep sigh would escape one on looking at the relic, that, unlike the harp of the son of Jesse, it was seldom or never tuned to allay an evil spirit, or to celebrate the glorious grace of the Messiah's reign.

SECTION II.

DUBLIN SUBJECT TO THE ENGLISH PAPAL RULE.

We have mentioned that the Danes of Dublin exchanged heathenism for Christianity, in its Roman form, about the year 948.

The Black Book of Christ Church has the following account of the origin of that edifice:—
"Sitricus, king of Dublin, son of Ableb, earl of Dublin, gave to the Blessed Trinity, and to Donate, first bishop of Dublin, a place on which to build a church of the Blessed Trinity, where the arches or vaults were founded, with the following lands, viz. : Beal-duleck, [now Baldoyle,] Rechen, Portrahern, with their villeins, cows, and corn : he also contributed gold and silver enough wherewith to build the church and the whole court thereof." The "arches or vaults" are thought to have been places which had been used for storing merchandise, though others conjecture that they were rather cells for devotion. Donate became bishop of Dublin in 1038, and died in 1074. The Church of the Holy Trinity, erected by him as above, afterwards became Christ Church Cathedral. He also built the Chapel of St. Michael, which, in course of time, was changed into a parish-church.

It is probable that the Danes of Dublin received their Christianity from England, by communication with ecclesiastics in that country. Indications of connection with Rome, through Canterbury, are not wanting in the case of Bishop Donate; but that connection becomes apparent in the case of Donate's successor, Patrick. Sir James Ware, in his "Bishops of Ireland," gives the letter which the king of Dublin sent with Patrick to Lanfranc, the English primate, requesting his consecration, as having been chosen by the clergy and citizens to be their bishop. Ware gives also the formal vow of canonical obedience which Patrick made to Lanfranc and his successors. Ware furnishes likewise two letters which Patrick brought back with him from Lanfranc—one to Godfrid, king of Dublin, and the other to Tirdelvac, king of Ireland: both of them written in that complimentary, patronizing, admonitory, and hortatory strain, which dignified ecclesiastics of those days, as of our own, well knew how to employ for their purposes, in addressing secular lords. This Tirdelvac is the same king to whom, as Lanigan mentions, Pope Gregory VII., Hildebrand, sent a letter, "much in the style of several others which he wrote to several kings, princes, etc., for the purpose of claiming not only a spiritual, but likewise a temporal and political superiority over all the kingdoms and principalities of Europe. Having insinuated his claim over Ireland, he concludes with giving directions to Tirdelvac, etc., to refer to him whatever affairs the settling of which may require his assistance." Thus did the pope's temporal power over nations and their rulers come in, as it were by stealth, behind his spiritual power. And as it was in the days of Hildebrand, so it is in those of Pio Nono.

Usher, in his "Religion of the Ancient Irish," gives the following letter from Henry I. of England to his primate, ordering the consecration of a Dublin bishop, in 1121: "Henry, king of England, to Ralph, archbishop of Canterbury, greeting. The king of Ireland hath intimated unto me by his writ, and the burgesses of Dublin, that they have chosen this Gregory for their bishop, and send him unto you to be consecrated. Wherefore, I wish you, that satisfying their requests, you perform his consecration without delay. Witness—Ranulph, our chancellor at Windsor." Usher writes that "all the burgesses of Dublin, likewise, and the whole assembly of the clergy, directed their joint letters to the archbishop of Canterbury at the same time: wherein, among other things, they write thus: 'Know you for verity that the bishops of Ireland have great indignation towards us, and that bishop most of all that dwelleth at Armagh, because we will not obey their ordination, but will always be under your government.'" Hence it appears what an opposition existed between the Irish and Romanist ecclesiastics of the country. The expression used by the Dublin burgesses and clergy is even stronger than Usher has rendered it: "*maximum zelum erga nos*"—"the greatest indignation towards us." The "indignation" was not less in the Romanists against the Irish.

There were essential ecclesiastical differences between the two. The Irish churches were self-governed—owning no subjection to the pope. They freely followed each its own mode of worship: none of them used the Roman. Each church had its bishop: so much so that Roman divines censured Ireland for its "paganism" in having as many bishops as churches. The Irish clergy were not bound to celibacy; for among rules given for their style of dress, one is that their wives should have their heads veiled when they walk abroad. The Irish churches were charged by Romanists with not observing due order in ordaining bishops: in England, indeed, and on the Continent, the ministry of Irish-ordained clergy was often disallowed. The Roman laws with regard to matrimony, the use of chrism in baptism, and the observance of Easter, were not recognized by the Irish Christians. These differences gave rise to strong contentions when the parties came in contact elsewhere; and no doubt the bishops of Ireland looked upon the bishop of Dublin placing himself in the position of a suffragan to Canterbury, instead of being in fellowship with themselves, as the inhabitants of a besieged city would on a person who sought to open its gates to the foe.

The jurisdiction of the Dublin bishop did not extend beyond the city. Limerick and Waterford were each of them a bishop's see; and being, like Dublin, Danish settlements, their prelates were of the Roman order, and suffragans of Canterbury. Gregory, whose application for consecration we have mentioned, lived to see the long-cherished wishes of the pope and his English primate consummated, in all the Irish churches being placed as one under the sway of Rome.

Early in the twelfth century, one Gillebert, who, as Lanigan thinks, had been ordained among the Irish, was invited by the people of Limerick to become their bishop. This changed his ecclesiastical relation, and he became intimate with Anselm, the archbishop of Canterbury. He took a journey to the continent, and was enamored with the Roman worship, as there celebrated. It occurred to him how much more orderly and respectable the Irish clergy and ritual would be, were they brought into conformity with Rome. The pope eventually made him his legate for Ireland, and he wrote more than one treatise in furtherance of his favorite purpose. "It is probable," writes Lanigan, "that Gillebert was encouraged in his proceedings by Anselm, although it can scarcely be supposed that Anselm supplied him with his bad arguments." The same author adds, "Gillebert did not succeed, at least to any considerable degree, in setting aside the Irish offices." But the leaven spread. Malachi, bishop of Armagh, successor to the one alluded to in the Dublin letter which we have quoted above from Usher, entered into Gillebert's views, and went to Rome to solicit two "palls"—one for Armagh, and the other for Cashel—making them *arch*bishoprics. The pope received him graciously, appointed him legate for Ireland instead of Gillebert, who had become infirm through age, and promised that the palls should be granted on their being applied for in due form, by delegates from a council of the clergy and chief men of the country. A council was held on Malachi's return, and ultimately Pope Eugenius sent Cardinal Paparo to Ireland, who conferred *four* palls: namely, one each upon Armagh, Dublin, Cashel, and Tuam. Thus all Ireland was brought into direct fellowship with the pope, and vowed allegiance to him as her head. Dublin also ceased to be ecclesiastically subject to Canterbury, and became itself an archiepiscopal see. Then, or in a few years afterwards, several bishoprics in the neighborhood of the city, as Clondalkin, Tallaght, Taney, etc., were merged in the see of Dublin.

The movement commenced by Gillebert had other than spiritual results. Within four years after Ireland received the palls, Henry II., king of England, obtained from Pope Adrian IV., as absolute sovereign of Ireland in his capacity of vicar of Christ, a bull, formally assigning over the country to Henry and his successors on the throne of England as its lords. The grant was made by the pope to the king "for extending the borders of the Church, restraining the progress of vice, for the correction of manners, the planting of virtue, and the increase of religion." It empowered Henry to "enter Ireland, and execute therein whatever shall pertain to the honor of God and the welfare of the land." It enjoined the people to "receive him honorably, and reverence him as their lord: the rights of their churches still remaining inviolate." It bound Henry and his successors to pay to the pope one penny annually for each house in the country. It concluded by exhorting Henry to fulfil his mission for the good of Ireland, that he " might be entitled to the fullness of eternal reward from God, and obtain a glorious crown on earth throughout all ages." This bull from Adrian was variously confirmed by his successors on the papal throne.

Henry was too much occupied otherwise to act upon this bull at once. In the mean time, preparations were being made for his success, and no doubt the connection which had existed between Dublin and Canterbury favored his interests among the Danes in the former city. In 1162, Dermod, king of Leinster, brought these Danes and their king under his own power. Five years afterwards, O'Connor, king of Ireland, made war on Dermod and the Danes. Dermod, reduced to extremity, applied to the king of England for aid to regain his territories. Henry issued warrants to his subjects, commanding them to furnish Dermod with supplies. The principal person who espoused his cause was the Earl of Pembroke, surnamed "Strongbow," from his power in archery. To engage this lord in his interest, the king of Leinster promised him his daughter in marriage, and his crown in reversion. Strongbow came accordingly, and Dermod recovered his lost possessions, made himself master of Dublin, and appointed Miles de Cogan, an English adventurer, commander of the place. Dermod died in 1171, and Strongbow became king of Leinster, including its metropolis, Dublin. Henry, hearing of his success, became jealous; but the earl visited England, and appeased Henry's wrath by consenting to surrender Dublin to him, and to hold the province under him as liege-lord.

In October, 1172, Henry himself crossed the channel from Milford to Waterford, with a fleet of two hundred and forty vessels, bringing with him many of his court and nobility, four hundred knights or men-at-arms, and four thousand soldiers. On landing, he received the submission of the English settlers: Strongbow did homage to him for the crown of Leinster; and, in his progress towards Dublin, many of the Irish princes offered him their allegiance. At Dublin, Strongbow formally ceded the city to him, and he appointed Hugh de Lacy its governor, who bore the titles of bailiff, seneschal, and guardian or custos: under the Danes, its chief magistrate had been called "Mor Maer," *Great Steward*. Henry then went southward, and attended an ecclesiastical council at Cashel, wherein all matters affecting the Irish churches were arranged according to the will of the Roman pontiff. On returning to the metropolis, he gave the laws of England to his Irish subjects, held a parliament, and established courts of Chancery, King's Bench, Common Pleas, and Exchequer, on the model of those in London. Henry spent his Christmas in Dublin, with truly royal feasting and splendor. There being no place in the city large enough for his use, he " caused to be erected a royal palace, framed artificially of wattles, according to the custom of the country," on a spot outside the walls, where Dame lane enters George's street. This palace " was a long pavilion, like a cabin, which, being well-furnished with plate, household stuff, and good cheer, made a better appearance than ever had been before seen in Ireland. Many of the Irish princes flocked thither to pay their duty to the king, not without admiration and applause of his magnificence." His object herein was to establish his power in the country by attaching the chiefs and people to himself, giving proofs of his good will towards them in order to secure theirs in return. Before his departure, at Easter, he granted the city of Dublin to the people of Bristol: " Wherefore," says the charter, " I will and firmly command that they do inhabit it, and hold it of me and of my heirs, well and in peace, freely and quietly, fully, and amply, and honorably, with all liberties and free customs which the men of Bristol have at Bristol, and through my whole land."

Earl Strongbow died in 1177, and was buried with great solemnity in Christ Church cathedral, where a monument was placed to his memory, which still exists, though much injured and defaced. The record of his death states that he was interred "in sight of the cross." Happy had it been if all who undertook the cure of souls, in those and other times, had been as concerned that men should know the doctrine of the cross for their salvation while living, as the ecclesiastics who arranged the obsequies of Strongbow were to lay his corpse within view of the crucifix, which the spirit of Antichrist has substituted as a refuge for the soul in the place of a living faith in Christ!

During the time that the English power was being established in Ireland, the archbishopric of Dublin was held by the celebrated Lawrence O'Toole. At first he opposed Henry's projects, but afterwards acquiesced in them. We read of him, that although he studiously avoided all popular applause, yet his charity to the poor, and hospitality to the rich, could not be concealed. He caused every day, sometimes sixty, sometimes forty, and at least thirty poor men to be fed in his presence, besides many whom he otherwise relieved. He entertained the rich splendidly and elegantly, with variety of dishes, and several sorts of wines, yet never tasted of the repast himself, contented with coarser fare. In 1179, he attended the second general council of the Lateran, and while there obtained a bull from the Pope Alexander, confirming the dioceses of Glendalough, Kildare, Ferns, Leighlin, and Ossory, to his metropolitan see.

When Cardinal Paparo gave palls to Armagh and Dublin, he did not sufficiently appoint in what relation the two sees should stand to each other. To Comyn, who followed O'Toole in that of Dublin, Pope Honorius III. granted that he should be primate in his archdiocese, and that no prelate should have jurisdiction over him therein, save the pope or his legates. A controversy of some centuries' duration arose between Dublin and Armagh on this subject. The sign of primatial rank and prerogative consisted in the cross

of the prelate being carried upright before him.
Popes, councils, parliaments, were variously appealed to, and gave judgment variously. On one occasion, the archbishop of Armagh appeared at Howth with his cross erect, which some belonging to the Dublin party observing, they beat it down and drove him out of Leinster. At another time the archbishop of Armagh came to a parliament in Dublin, under the king's warrant that he should have no molestation; but the archbishop of Dublin would not allow him to appear, because he insisted on having his cross carried upright. In 1345, Fitz-Ralph, of Armagh, procured from King Edward III. authority to bear his cross erect in any part of Ireland. Accordingly he came to Dublin, and remained in the city three days, exhibiting the symbol of preëminence, asserting his claim, publicly reading the bulls of popes in support of it, and denouncing excommunication against any who should oppose it. Hewson, the lord justice, the prior of Kilmainham, and other high officials, interfered, (being induced to do so, it is said, by a bribe from the archbishop of Dublin,) and put a stop to those proceedings. Fitz-Ralph left the city in great anger. On reaching Drogheda he pronounced the curse of the Church on the parties who had dared to impugn his dignity. This alarmed and humbled them. The Kilmainham prior himself, seized with dangerous illness, sent deputies to confess his sin, and implore absolution. He died before their return, and his remains were refused Christian burial; but the grace desired being at length

vouchsafed, they were then allowed a resting-place in consecrated ground. The next archbishop of Dublin received letters from Edward, revoking those given to Fitz-Ralph, on the ground that the latter had been obtained through misrepresentation. Finally, Pope Innocent VI. brought the dispute to a close, by ordaining that Armagh should be primate of all Ireland, and Dublin primate of Ireland, answering to the difference, ecclesiastically, between Canterbury and York in England.

We must now retrace our steps, and notice matters which, in order to avoid breaking the thread of our narrative, we refrained from alluding to before.

The establishment of the abbey of St. Mary, on the north side of the Liffey, and the building of the church of the Holy Trinity, or Christ Church, and that of St. Michael, in the heart of the city, have been mentioned. In 1095, the church of St. Michan was founded between Ostmantown and Mary's Abbey, by a Dane of that name; and about a century later, archbishop Comyn demolished the old parochial church of St. Patrick, and erected and endowed a cathedral in its place. In 1146, the nunnery of St. Mary de Hoggins was built not far from the eastern gate of the city, which thence took the name of Dame's Gate, and the memorial of the nunnery is still preserved in the names Dame street and Dame lane. Twenty years later, the great monastery of All-Hallows was erected where Trinity College now stands; and in the same year was also founded the priory of All-Hallows, at Hoggin's-green, now called Stephen's-green: both the monastery and the priory sprang from the zeal of Dermod, king of Leinster. About the same time, St. Andrew's church was built where the Cattle Market is at present. The abbey of St. Thomas was erected by Fitz-Audelin, butler to Henry II., and its situation is yet known as Thomas court, and Thomas street: it was, however, then "near" Dublin. Earl Strongbow erected the priory of Knights' Templars at Kilmainham, where now stands the Royal Hospital: their grounds extended across the river, including a portion of the Phœnix Park. In 1188, the priory of St. John the Baptist was built by Alured de Palmer, on what is, in our day, the north side of Thomas street. And, in 1202, William Marshall, earl of Pembroke, established the priory of St. Saviour, on the site of the present Four Courts. In 1235, the abbey of St. Francis was erected, and from it afterwards was taken the name of Francis street. In 1259, the monastery of the Holy Trinity was founded by Earl Talbot, where Crow street theatre stood in modern time. The abbey of Witeschan, for Friars Penitent, was founded near the Coombe in 1268; and ten years later the monastery of Carmelites, or White Friars, was founded by Sir Robert Bagot, near the present Whitefriars street. The churches of St. Nicholas Within, St. Werburgh's, St. Owen's, (now Audoen's,) and St. Catharine's, are believed to have existed at that period. So that the Dublin of the thirteenth century must have been well supplied with ecclesiastical buildings. Some of these establishments had immense property, and their heads were lords of parliament, who had great influence in political affairs.

The "wall and tower" with which the Danes encompassed Dublin for its defence when they first became masters of it, were, of course, built of masonry, probably, however, of a somewhat rude and frail kind, a step or two in advance upon the "forts" which universal tradition ascribes to them, and which are so frequently met with in the country. In the year 1000, they repaired and added to the fortifications, which then became of considerable strength. The city wall went, it is believed, from Cork Hill on the east down to within some distance of the river, then along, or rather above, the present Cook street, running up the hill through Owen's or Audoen's Arch, and afterwards, a few yards below the top of the rise on the south side, took its course eastward till it reached Cork Hill. There were several gates: one on the east, called Dame's Gate; another towards the west, called Owen's Gate; a third on the north, or north-west, near the present Winetavern street, leading to the river; and a fourth on the south side. Early in the thirteenth century, it was judged that the city required greater security; and on a representation made to that effect by Meyler Fitz-Henry, the lord justice, or, as the English would say, the lord lieutenant, king John granted him a commission to "erect a castle there, in such competent place as he should judge most expedient, as well to curb the city as to defend it, if occasion should so require, and to make it as strong as he could with good and durable walls." It was, if so much could be accomplished, to be a "palace" as well as a "castle." To aid the work, John assigned to Fitz-Henry a debt of three hundred marks (£200) due to the king by one Jeffrey Fitz-Robert. He also ordered the inhabitants to improve the city defences, to defray the cost of which he appointed them an annual fair to be held for eight days, beginning on the festival of the "Invention of the Holy Cross." It is thought that the "castle" was finished by the archbishop Henry Loundres, in 1220. It was built on the site occupied by its present successor. The entrance to it was on its north side, from what is called, in consequence, "Castle street," and was secured by two towers, a portcullis, and a drawbridge. What now forms the Lower Castle Yard and parts adjoining, were then called "Sheep's Land," (whence *Ship* street,) and a lodgment of water there was called the "City Ditch." In 1215, the citizens obtained a royal license to build a bridge over the Liffey where they pleased. The site chosen was probably where we have conjectured the old Ford to have been; and from this bridge the street leading to it from the city naturally came to be called "Bridge street." "High street," named from its position, was burned down in 1285, and the year following the greater part of the city was consumed. It is recorded to the honor of the inhabitants, that they first made a collection to repair the damage done to Christ Church, "before they thought of reëdifying their own houses."

The reader has been informed that Henry II. gave special encouragement to his loving subjects of Bristol to settle in Dublin. A gloomy event followed in connection with their having taken advantage of his permission. Easter Monday, ordinarily accounted bright, acquired the name of "Black Monday." "The occasion of Black Monday," writes Ware in his "Antiquities," anno 1209, "and the original remembrance thereof, arose in Dublin. The city of Dublin, by reason of some great mortality, being waste and desolate, the inhabitants of Bristol flocked thither to dwell, who, after their country manner upon holy-days, some for love of the fresh air, some to avoid idleness, some other for pastime, pleasure, and gaming sake, flocked out of the town towards Cullen's Wood upon Monday in Easter-week. The Beirnes and Tooles, (the mountain enemies,) like wolves, lay in ambush for them, and upon finding them unarmed, fell upon them, and slew three hundred men, besides women and children which they led in their hands. Although, shortly after, the town was upon the report thereof soon peopled again by Bristolians, yet that dismal day is yearly remembered, and solemnly observed by the mayor, sheriffs, and citizens, with feast and banquet, and pitching of tents in that place, in most brave sort, daring the enemy upon his peril not to be so hardy as ever to approach near their feasting camp." This custom was continued for some centuries. At last, on Easter Monday, in 1578, "the wind and rain were so violent that neither bowmen nor shot could go abroad;" and brave as the then chief magistrate and his compeers might be to face the *human* "mountain enemies," they shrank from encountering the terrible war of elements. Nor did their valorous successors in following years, except on one occasion, ever feel called upon to resume this old champion-like celebration of "Black Monday."

In the latter half of the thirteenth century, warm contests arose between the spiritual and the civic rulers of the city. So excessive were the "dues" exacted by the clergy for church services and purposes, that it was resolved to limit their power and reduce their demands. This incensed the archbishop Fulk de Sandford. He excommunicated the mayor and other secular officials, placed the city under an interdict, and had the inhabitants denounced by the pope's legate then in London. In 1268, Sir Robert de Ufford, the lord justice, brought about an adjustment. Among the terms agreed upon were the following:—If a citizen were guilty of a public sin, he might commute its punishment for a sum of money: if he persisted in it, and it were great and public, he was to be *cudgelled* (*fustigetur*) about the church: on that proving insufficient to reform him, he was to be *cudgelled* before the processions made to the cathedrals; and in case he was still impenitent, he was to be expelled the city or *cudgelled* through it. The modern use of the horsewhip in Ireland, for administering Romanist pastoral discipline, might refer to the above agreement as its precedent.

Honorable mention is made of John le Dacer,

the first "provost" of Dublin, as having been a great public benefactor. Besides building two chapels and granting other liberalities to the Church, he provided a marble cistern for the city conduit, such as had never been seen before: he also erected a new bridge over the Liffey, and in a time of scarcity sent out three ships and brought over a supply of corn, bestowing one cargo on the lord justice and the militia, and a second on the Dominican and Augustin friars, reserving the third for the exercise of his own hospitality and bounty. The last-named generosity probably occurred in 1310, for we are told that in that year the bakers of Dublin were drawn on hurdles at the tails of horses, through the streets, for using false weights and for other malpractices, during a famine when a "crannoch" of wheat (four Winchester bushels) sold for twenty shillings, the price in England a few years before (1288) having been only fourpence per bushel. Another famine occurred in 1331, when the distress of the citizens was singularly "relieved by a prodigious shoal of fish, called 'turleyhides,' being cast on shore at the mouth of the Dodder. They were from thirty to forty feet long, and so thick that men standing on each side one of them could not see those on the other. Upwards of two hundred of them were killed by the people."

Besides famine, pestilence frequently made havoc in the city. One that occurred in 1348 carried off "vast numbers"—a writer of the time says, "fourteen thousand!" A second came in 1361; a third, yet more destructive, in 1370;

and a fourth in 1383, which "destroyed abundance of people." Of one in 1439, "three thousand" persons died; of another in 1447, "vast multitudes died." What was the state of medical practice in Dublin during the times we are speaking of cannot be satisfactorily ascertained; but a statement in Messrs. Warburton, Whitelaw, and Walsh's History, may suggest to us that the healing art was studied among the Irish and in Dublin at even an earlier period. "In passing," say the authors, "through Mitre alley, an obscure part of the old city, near St. Patrick's Cathedral, the eye is attracted by an angular sign-board projecting from the wall, on which is the following inscription, 'Domestic medicine prescribed from Irish manuscripts,' and a couplet of Irish poetry, which is literally, 'O Christ, the sick relieve: to their aid I Thee implore.' Attracted by this notice, we visited the doctor, in the hope of meeting those Irish manuscripts from which he derived his prescriptions. Nor were we disappointed. We found an old man of a genuine Milesian aspect, possessed of seventy-three very old and valuable volumes of vellum, bound in modern covers. They contained several thousand recipes in Latin and Irish, written in a very beautiful but very old Irish character. The title-pages were wanting, but they were supposed to be a collection of native and other recipes made in the thirteenth century, and from that period traditionally descending from family to family."

Dublin had no school of learning after she became Roman, previous to the fourteenth century.

In 1313, Archbishop Leck obtained from Pope Clement V. a bull for founding "the university of scholars at Dublin," and in seven years more his successor, Bicknor, procured another bull from Pope John XXII., renewing and confirming the former. Bicknor applied himself with much spirit to perfect the design. The rules of this college are given by Ware. It had power to confer degrees, and at its opening several persons received that of doctor in divinity, and Rodiart, dean of St. Patrick's, was made doctor in canon law and chancellor of the university. It was held in St. Patrick's Cathedral. King Edward III. appointed for the university a professor of divinity, enlarged the original endownent, and by special writ granted his protection and safe conduct to the students while going and returning. It had, however, only a feeble and hardly-sustained existence. A vigorous attempt was made to revive it in 1496, when Archbishop Fitz-Simons, at a council held in Christ Church, "assigned certain stipends to the lecturers in the university at Dublin, payable yearly by himself and his suffragans." But we hear nothing of it afterwards.

In Bicknor's day, indolence and mendicancy seem to have been rampant in Dublin, and he laudably sought to promote industry as well as learning among the people. There was formerly "extant in the registry of St. Mary's Abbey an account of a remarkable sermon preached by him in Christ Church, against sloth and idleness; wherein he bitterly complained of the mischiefs arising from the strangers and beggars who infested the city and suburbs of Dublin; and so warm was he in his discourse, that he cursed every one that would not exercise some trade or calling every day, more or less. His sermon had such an influence that the then mayor of Dublin exercised his authority on the occasion, and would not suffer any person within his liberties but such as spun or knitted as they walked the streets. Even the begging friars were not excused." The evils thus rebuked and corrected came to the metropolis from the provinces, where we have reason to believe they prevailed a century and a half later. King Henry VII. inquired of Fitz-Simon, archbishop of Dublin, when the latter waited on him at court, why his Irish subjects so often rebelled and made no improvement under the English rule, notwithstanding the advantages which the country afforded. Fitz-Simon referred the king to an explanation he had sent to his majesty in a letter some time before, ascribing the poverty and discontent of the Irish to their "idleness." Let us rejoice that, whatever may have been the facts of the case then, a disposition towards industry and self-reliance is now growing up rapidly among the people, and that they are, in all parts of the country, coming to regard it as a maxim of common sense and an element of social prosperity, not less than an ordinance of God's word and a principle of his providence, that "If any will not work, neither shall he eat."

Edward Bruce, brother to the celebrated Robert, king of Scotland, invaded the north of Ireland about the year 1315, marched thence towards Dublin, and, encamping at Castleknock, placed the city in imminent danger. The citizens, to protect themselves, burned some of the suburbs on the west, and, besides other additions to their defences, they built a new wall on the north side of the town, along what is now Merchant's Quay, about four hundred feet nearer the river than the old line. Bruce burned St. Mary's Abbey and plundered St. Patrick's Cathedral, but observing that the city was well prepared to stand a siege, he withdrew towards Naas. Less than a century afterwards, the citizens returned the visit of the Scots; for, in June, 1405, they fitted out a fleet and "invaded Scotland at St. Ninian's," where their forces "behaved themselves valiantly and did much mischief." They subsequently sailed down the channel and committed some depredations on the coast of Wales, bringing back with them the shrine of St. Cubie, which trophy they deposited among the relics in Christ Church. For the great services thus rendered by the citizens in creating division among his enemies the Scots and Welsh, King Henry IV. granted that the mayor of Dublin should thenceforth have a gilt sword borne before him, for the honor of the king and his heirs, as was customary with the mayor of London.

Feuds and disaffections prevailing in Ireland, to the weakening, if not peril, of the English power there, King Richard II. had funds for visiting that country placed at his disposal by his clergy and parliament. At Michaelmas, 1394, he landed at Waterford with four thousand men-at-arms and thirty thousand archers, the duke of Gloucester, the earls of Nottingham and Rutland, and other of his nobility, accompanying him. To give gorgeousness to his state, he brought with him his crown jewels. Not fewer than seventy-five Irish chiefs, each bearing the title of "king," waited upon him in Dublin and humbly tendered their submissions. They were perfectly charmed with his royal pomp and hospitality, and perhaps were yet more pleasurably excited by the condescending notices to which so great a potentate admitted them, for Richard and his courtiers conversed with them, through Castile, one of his attendants, and the Earl of Ormond, both of whom understood the Irish language. The four principal princes were treated with marked favor above the rest. They were informed that his majesty was disposed to confer upon them the order of knighthood. But, in their simplicity, they did not at first understand the value of this grace, and they expressed some surprise that knighthood should be considered any addition to the rank they already held. "Every Irish king," they said, "makes his son a 'knight' at seven years old, or, in case of his death, the next kinsman. We assemble," they continued, "in a plain: the candidates run with slender lances against a shield fastened on a stake: he who breaks the greatest number is distinguished by particular honors attached to his new dignity." Richard and his great men acknowledged such proofs of early prowess to be highly praiseworthy; but it was explained that all the states of Europe adopted a more solemn form in bestowing knightly honor. The ceremonial was described in detail, and the four Irish princes, being now able to appreciate the boon, accepted it with due thanks at Richard's hand, in Christ Church Cathedral, March 25th, 1395, after which these royal personages, thus exalted above their former selves, appeared in robes of state, and were seated at the king's table. Richard having spent nine months in Ireland, was hurried home by information from the archbishop of York and the bishop of London, that in England religion and the Church were in much danger through the spread of Lollardism. The prelates told him that the reformers had gone so far as to make appeals to the parliament, and that that body had received them with a degree of attention that greatly alarmed the clergy, so that the king's own piety and authority alone could save the faith from utter ruin.

Notwithstanding the great spread of Wycliffe's doctrines in England, few traces exist of their having found their way into Dublin, which is the more remarkable from the constant communication which was kept up between that country and the Irish metropolis. But there is evidence that about the time of Wycliffe's birth (1324) opinions the reverse of what were deemed orthodox existed in the city. In the year 1327, "Adam Duffe O'Toole was convicted of blasphemy in Dublin, namely, for denying the incarnation of

Christ, the Trinity in unity; for affirming that the blessed Virgin was an harlot; that there was no resurrection; that the Scriptures were a mere fable, and that the apostolical see was an imposture and usurpation; and the next year, pursuant to his sentence, was burned on Hoggin Green, near Dublin." It is not unlikely that this man held Waldensian principles; if so, persons acquainted with the representations made of those tenets by Romanist writers, well know what weight is to be attached to the charge of denying the Incarnation, the Trinity, and the inspiration of the Scriptures.

Shortly before this trial and execution of O'Toole, namely, in 1324, Lady Alice Kettle, William Outlaw, her son, and two other persons, are said to have been charged with "witchcraft and enchantments," in the spiritual court of Ossory; but another authority, judged by Ware to be more trustworthy, records that her ladyship suffered death for heresy, and that she was the first that was ever known to suffer for that crime in Ireland. The chief magistrate of Kilkenny favored the delinquents. His bishop, Ledred, accused him of heresy, excommunicated him, and had him committed to the castle in Dublin. The prior of Kilmainham, however, then lord justice, treated him kindly. The bishop, enraged, went to Dublin, and there charged "heresy" upon the lord justice. A parliament was summoned, who appointed a committee of inquiry. "They examined the witnesses apart, and every one of them made oath that the justice was orthodox, a zealous champion

of the faith, and ready to defend it with his life.
Upon this report of the committee he was solemnly
acquitted, and prepared a sumptuous banquet for
all his defenders." A year or two subsequently,
Ledred was himself accused of heresy by his
metropolitan, Bicknor, and appealed to the judgment of the pope, who exempted him from Bicknor's jurisdiction. We have no means of knowing
certainly what the "heresy" was which parties
thus charged upon each other. It may have involved no very serious departure from the faith
received and enforced by the Romish Church;
but, on the other hand, it may have been a near
approach to evangelical truth. At all events,
after Bicknor's death, Pope Clement VI. sent a
commission to the new archbishop "to make inquisition against all such heretics as had fled from
the prosecution of Richard Ledred, bishop of
Ossory, into the diocese of Dublin, and had been
protected by Alexander Bicknor, and to bring
them to due punishment according to the canons."

Bale, to whom we shall refer hereafter, in his
book entitled "The Great Process against Lord
Cobham," having noticed the act of the English
parliament, which declared Lollardism to be both
treason and heresy, and ordained that a convicted
Lollard should be first hung in chains for his
treason and then burned for his heresy, says that
"many were taken in divers quarters and suffered
most cruel deaths. And many fled out of the
land into Germany, Bohemia, France, Spain, Portugal, and into the Weld [*Wold*, open country]
of Scotland, Wales, and Ireland, working there

many marvels against their false kingdom too long to write." Hence it appears that some Lollards came to Ireland; but had they been in considerable numbers, or made much stir in favor of their principles, more information would have been preserved respecting them than has been handed down to our time.

In the year 1489, "musquets" were brought to Dublin from Germany, and six of them, as a great rarity, were presented to Gerald, Earl of Kildare, then lord deputy, which he put into the hands of his guards, as they stood sentinels before his house in Thomas court. They are supposed to have been the first firearms even seen in Ireland.

The impostor Simnel, who had been trained by an Oxford priest to personate the deceased Earl of Warwick, and claimed to be the rightful heir to the English throne, came to Dublin in 1486, and was received by the Earl of Kildare, then lord justice, and other chief officials, with all respect and submission, they being warm partisans of the house of York. He was crowned in Christ-Church, under the style of Edward VI. The crown used on the occasion was taken from the image of the Virgin in the nunnery of St. Mary, already mentioned, between the city gate and Hoggin's green, afterwards "College" green. But the year following, the cause of Simnel having become desperate, the mayor, Jenicho Marks, humbly besought mercy for himself and the citizens from King Henry VII., pleading in apology for their misdeeds the example that had been set them by the king's representative, the Archbishop of Dublin, and most of the clergy in the country except the Primate of Armagh. In June, 1488, Sir Richard Edgecumbe came with a royal commission to receive new oaths of fidelity from the lord deputy, with the nobility, clergy, and people who had been engaged in the revolt, and to grant them a full pardon. It may be observed, as indicating the state of education in the city at this period, that several of the parties who subscribed the application to the king for forgiveness, did so by affixing their mark to it, being unable to write.

Dublin, under Roman ecclesiastical rule, had its pageant performances on sacred days. The reader will form an idea of these exhibitions by the following outline of the provision for one in the procession on Corpus Christi festival: the account will also show the existence and names of the several city guilds. The glovers were to represent Adam and Eve, with an angel bearing a sword before them. The curriers, Cain and Abel, with an altar and their offering. The mariners and vintners, Noah and the persons in his ark, apparelled in the habit of carpenters and salmon-takers. The weavers personated Abraham and Isaac, with their offering and altar. The smiths, Pharaoh and his host. The skinners, the camel, with the children of Israel. The goldsmiths were to find the King of Cullen—(who was he?) The hoopers, or coopers, were to find the shepherds, with an angel singing *Gloria in excelsis Deo*. Corpus Christi guild was to find Christ in his passion, with the Maries and angels.

The tailors were to find Pilate with his fellowship, and his wife clothed accordingly. The barbers, Annas and Caiaphas. The fishers, the apostles. The merchants, the prophets. And the butchers, the tormentors. The reader may comment on the list as he will. Doubtless each corporation felt a gratification in doing its part well, though the degree of complacency must have varied according to the honor and excellency of what it had to personify.

What was reckoned an act of gross sacrilege was perpetrated in Dublin, early in the reign of Henry VIII. The partisans of the lord deputy Kildare, and those of the Earl of Ormond, met in St. Patrick's cathedral professedly for an amicable conference with a view to adjust differences which had led to much asperity between them. It was a stratagem, however, on the part of Ormond and his people to get Kildare and his followers into their power. Words soon gave place to blows. Some of the arrows of Kildare's men stuck in the images of the sacred edifice. The daring profanation was reported to the pope, who in his clemency absolved the citizens, but, "in detestation of the deed, and to keep up the memory of it for ever," ordained that "the mayor of Dublin should walk barefoot through the city in open procession before the sacrament on Corpus Christi day yearly"—a penance duly submitted to till the Reformation, and the performance of which must have given much interest to the festival.

The year 1535 saw Dublin in one of the greatest of its many perils. Fitzgerald, son of the lord deputy, was left in charge of it while his father went to England. A rumor was spread that the latter had been seized and beheaded in London. The son, on the 11th of June, came with a party of a hundred and forty horse, and made a formal and entire resignation of his authority to the chancellor, and then forthwith raised the standard of rebellion. He demanded liberty to pass through the city in order to besiege the castle, giving the magistrates some time to consider their reply. In this interval, a large supply of provisions and means of defence were conveyed into the castle. Alderman John Fitz-Simons, on his own account, furnished its commander with twenty-two tuns of wine, twenty-four of beer, two hundred dried ling, sixteen hogsheads of powdered beef, twenty chambers for mines, and an iron chain for the drawbridge, forged in his own house to avoid suspicion. The citizens then, with the commander's concurrence, agreed to Fitzgerald's demand, on the condition that no injury should be done to themselves. They had at first sent a messenger to the king for help, and he brought an encouraging answer. The rebels killed Archbishop Allen when he attempted to escape; and they broke faith with the citizens, by threatening to place some of the children of the latter on their works, to deter the garrison in the castle from firing upon the besiegers. The citizens at last closed their gates, imprisoning the soldiers who were within the walls, and cutting them off from their comrades outside. Fitzgerald was absent from his camp.

On hearing of what had occurred, he hastened back, attempted to take the city, but was repulsed and obliged to retire. The fidelity of the citizens was not unrewarded. The king, Henry VIII., by letters patent, dated February 4, 1538, after reciting the " siege, famine, miseries, wounds, and loss of blood," they had suffered, granted them " all the building and estates belonging to the dissolved monastery of All-hallows, near Dublin, lying in the counties of Dublin, Meath, Louth, Kildare, Tipperary, Kilkenny, and elsewhere in Ireland, at the rent of four pounds, four shillings, and three farthings." And, further, to repair the weakened and ruined great forts and towers of the city and its walls, he confirmed to them, for ever, a formal grant of nearly forty pounds a year, with an annual gift of twenty pounds from himself.

The hill on which Dublin stood was not yet entirely cleared of the "hazel-wood" which at first gave it the name of "Ath-Cliath," for the annals record that during the quarrels between the two factions of Ormond and Kildare, the former "came down with a great host of Irishmen, and encamped in Thomas Court Wood." What is now Dame street was then an "avenue" leading from the city gate to Hogges, or Hoggin's, Green.

SECTION III.

DUBLIN DURING THE BRITISH REFORMATION.

The city had been for five hundred years under the spiritual yoke of Romanism, and, during nearly four centuries out of the five, the secular power of England had, for upholding its own interests, been joined with that spiritual dominion in both countries. In profound yet contented servitude to the pope, Ireland remained till Henry VIII. had numbered more than thirty years on the English throne. Continental Europe had been convulsed throughout: the monk of Wittemberg had made the Vatican quake to its foundations: Great Britain was in the midst of the tumult attending a revolution in her faith; but Ireland slumbered on, as if drugged to stolidity or death under the pontiff's sway. Having little intercourse with other nations, she was so engrossed with the local interests and strifes of her people, that she neither cared for nor knew much of what was passing elsewhere. Many of the Irish clergy, some even of prelatic rank, were ignorant, indolent, and immoral; and occasionally their exactions were painfully oppressive. But the clergy were considered the almoners of grace, and the lords of conscience, and it was believed that in proportion to the amount of "carnal things" demanded by the Church, and to the cheerfulness with which those demands were acquiesced in, would be the degree of heavenly benediction vouchsafed from the "holy mother" to her much-loved and much-loving children. Priest-ridden as the latter were, the want of self-respect and self-reliance, the want of manly independent thought and action, the habit of hanging upon others and succumbing to them, which Popery generates, tended to keep the population at ease and even satisfied beneath the sacerdotal yoke. Clerical influence then, as now, beguiled Irish patriotism to believe that English rule was the incubus to be got rid of in order to uplift the people, and that the papal supremacy must be clung to as the only protecting and sustaining agency that could deliver from what was denounced as a usurped and crushing tyranny. Little did its victims think that the papal supremacy was itself the chief tyranny.

When, therefore, Ireland first heard of the "Reformation," the intelligence stirred no kindling sympathy in her heart. Previous movements had more or less prepared other countries to welcome it. England had had its Wycliffe: Bohemia, its Huss and Jerome: Switzerland had its Zuingle: Germany, its Luther: France, its Calvin: Scotland, its Knox. But in Ireland no herald had come to prepare the way of the Lord: no native champion had arisen there to assert His claims upon her homage: no Irishman ventured to raise a banner for his brethren to rally round and escape from their Babylonian thrall : no Irishman lifted his voice to warn his brethren of the "mystery of iniquity" that bewitched them, and to proclaim to them the "mystery of godliness" which brings freedom and health, and life for evermore. What was at first, and for not a short time afterwards, done to make Ireland Protestant, was for the most part effected by the English government obliging the clergy and laity to adopt the English ritual, as an obedience due to the king's will, and to be enforced by the king's authority. The project was dealt with as a matter of state-regimen more than of conscience towards God. The aim was rather to secure conformity of "bodily exercise" with outward regulations, than to renew the spirit to the faith of Christ; and this conformity was sought by the application of pains and penalties, more than by the intelligent and kind persuasions of Christianity. Happily, there has been since learned "a more excellent way."

When Henry received the crown, he was a zealous Romanist. Some dozen years afterwards came forth his book on the Seven Sacraments, written against Luther, and which obtained for him and his successors, from the pope, the title of "Defender of the Faith." In course of time, he found it convenient to repudiate the papacy of Rome, and appropriate its prerogatives to himself over his own realm. But Romanism was still to be the religion of his country; the principal change being that he who was its sovereign was to be its pope also. Cardinal Wolsey, when legate, had seized forty monasteries, and applied their properties to found a new college at Oxford. Henry judged that he could now do at his pleasure what Wolsey had done; and he disposed of the religious houses and estates in his kingdom according to his royal will and pleasure. That he still designed no change of creed, except in the matter of supremacy, is evident from the act passed by his parliament, and called the "Bloody Bill," which, by its first provision, consigned any party who denied the "real presence" to death by burning, and allowed no mitigation of the sentence even if the heresy were solemnly abjured. After Henry's marriage with Catherine Parr, in 1543, he became less hostile to the reformers. But it was not till the accession of his son, Edward VI., that the royalty of England became truly engaged for Protestantism. Next arose Mary, and, with her, Romanism returned to the high place from which it had been expelled. She was followed by Elizabeth, when a "uniformity" which excluded Romanism and often tried to annihilate English Puritanism, was affirmed, and was continued under her successor, James I.

It may be thought that the contents of the foregoing paragraphs are foreign to our subject—that they concern England, Ireland, and the Reformation, rather than Dublin. But the well-informed reader is aware how much proceedings about religion bore on the affairs of the city, and how closely the history of Ireland's metropolis is interwoven with that of Ireland itself, and of England also.

George Brown, provincial of the Augustinians

in England, was consecrated archbishop of Dublin, in March, 1535, in the place of Allen, whose murder has been already noticed. He was appointed a commissioner for abolishing the pope's supremacy, and establishing that of the king in Ireland. The task, however, proved greater than he was equal to, in consequence of the devotedness of the Irish clergy to the Roman pontiff. He advised the lord Cromwell that a parliament should be convened to carry the measure, which was done in the year following, when Brown proposed the act for establishing the king's supremacy, "in a short speech," setting forth that kings were head over all in their dominions, that even Christ paid tribute to Cæsar, and that kings and emperors, in the early ages of the Church, governed bishops and even popes themselves. Lord Brabazon seconded Brown's proposal, and it was adopted. The pope was quickly apprised of this, and sent over a bull of excommunication against all who should acknowledge Henry's claim, and great numbers of the clergy and laity, English as well as Irish, set themselves against it. However, through many difficulties, Henry's government kept its stand in Dublin and in the country.

On the 13th of June, 1541, another parliament met in Dublin, and ordained that henceforth Ireland should be made a "kingdom" instead of a "lordship," as hitherto, and that the king of England should be also "king" of Ireland. The contents of this statute were announced the next Sunday in St. Patrick's Cathedral, in presence of the lord deputy and many peers in their robes of state, with other principal persons ecclesiastical and secular. On that occasion, royal grace was exercised in pardoning and liberating prisoners. There were also great feastings, tournaments, and running at the ring on horseback, with grand civic processions in which the mayor bore the mace before the lord deputy; and the comedy of the "Nine Worthies" was acted for the entertainment of the citizens. The same parliament which gave to Henry the style and title of "king of Ireland," also confirmed to him the full and free disposal of all its abbeys and other religious houses, a power which he had already exercised upon some of those in and near Dublin.

It is said that Brown, before he left England to be made archbishop of Dublin, "advised the people to make their applications to Christ alone, for which doctrine he was much taken notice of." Probably his bias against the Roman opinions of mediation, inclined him to favor the king's supremacy. After coming to Ireland, he became yet more favorable to the reformed views. In 1538, he obtained a warrant for removing images and relics from his cathedrals, a measure which greatly provoked the Romanist party. But, though sincere, Brown had not the bold, God-trusting zeal, required in a reformer. He was fettered and enfeebled by his belief in the king's supremacy over the creed and the Church, and could not make any movement in favor of religion without sanction from the court.

Not until the fifth year of Edward VI. were decided steps taken towards introducing the reformed faith into Ireland. Under date of February 6, 1551, a royal order came to the lord deputy that the Church Liturgy, as it had been translated into English, should be used in the Irish churches. The order was laid before an assembly of the prelates and other leading clergy, called together in Dublin. Some of them were exasperated at the king's interference in Church affairs. Dowdal, the Armagh primate, threatened the deputy with the clergy's curse; and after warm contention, he and many others withdrew. Brown gave, as his reason for accepting the order, the duty of obeying his king. A proclamation was issued enjoining the use of the new liturgy, but it intimated no change in this prayer-book of King Edward from the old mass-book, except the circumstance of its being a translation into English. Public worship was first celebrated according to the new rubric, on Easter Sunday, in Christ Church Cathedral, before the lord deputy and other authorities. Few churches in the country adopted it. A new lord deputy endeavored to conciliate Dowdal, but in vain: so the primacy was withdrawn from Armagh and transferred to Dublin. Brown became primate of all Ireland; and Dowdal left the country, but did not formally vacate his archbishopric.

King Edward's prayer-book is believed to have been the first instance of printing in Ireland. Its title ran—"The Boke of common prayer and administracion of Sacramentes and other Rites and Ceremonies of the Churche after the use of the Churche of England. Dubliniæ, in officina

Humfredi Poweli, cum privilegio ad imprimendum solum. Anno Domini M.D.LI."

The government found it almost impossible to supply ecclesiastical vacancies with men of Protestant convictions. Two divines, however, came to Dublin in 1552, namely, Hugh Goodacre, appointed to Armagh, which Dowdal had abandoned though not resigned, and John Bale, appointed to Ossory. They were consecrated by Brown and other prelates, in Christ Church Cathedral, on the 2d of February. Brown and his assistants in the ceremony were for using the old Roman form on the occasion, lest, by adopting the English one, they should offend prejudice and create disturbance. Goodacre was willing to meet their wishes, but Bale, who was made of sterner stuff, would not consent. The point was yielded to him. He also required that the "altar" should be covered with a cloth as a "table," and that "nonprinted" bread, not the "wafer," should be had for the communion; and to his wishes in this respect Brown and his co-prelates had to give way. To their great surprise, no tumult ensued. Goodacre died in Dublin about three months afterwards: his death was ascribed to poison. Bale went to his charge, and of his ministry wrote:—
"My first proceedings were these: I earnestly exhorted the people to repentance for sin, and required them to give credit to the gospel of salvation; to acknowledge and believe that there was but one God, and him alone, without any other, sincerely to worship; to confess one Christ

for an only Saviour and Redeemer, and to trust in none other man's prayers, merits, nor yet deservings, but in his alone for salvation. I treated at large both of the heavenly and the political state of the Christian Church; and helpers I found none among my prebendaries and clergy, but adversaries a great number. I preached the gospel of the knowledge and right invocation of God. But when I once sought to destroy the idolatries and dissolve the hypocrites' yokes, then followed angers, slanders, and in the end slaughters of men." His labors in Ireland were of short duration, for on the death of Edward and accession of Mary he had to leave the kingdom; but he came back to England in Elizabeth's reign and joined the Puritans. Bale had studied at Cambridge, was a man of great learning, and the author of numerous works on theology and other subjects. He has been censured for his vehemence; and, in straightforward earnestness of purpose and endeavor, his habits presented a wide contrast to those of Brown; but he was not, as his censurers would have us to believe, more violent than Luther, Knox, and other leaders in the assault on Romanism in the sixteenth century. We may safely assume that the relative position of Popery and evangelism in Ireland would be far different from what it is, if, instead of indulging in lukewarmness, time-serving, and self-seeking, the parties professing the gospel had always cherished self-sacrificing earnestness like that of Bale, without his faults—faults probably more characteristic of the age than of the man. Lawrence Humfryd, dean of Winchester in 1550, no mean authority in the case, wrote of him:—

"Plurima Lutherus patefecit; Platina multa:
Quædam Vergerius; cuncta Balœus habet;"

which Harris translates, with more of rhyme than elegance, yet not without some spirit:—

"Platina hath much unveiled; but Luther more;
Vergerius many things; but Bale hath tore
Away the mask that pope and Popery wore."

The reader, it is hoped, requires no apology for this notice of such a man, though he was connected with Dublin only by two circumstances— his consecration there, as before stated, and his escape in a sailor's dress, on board a vessel there, when he fled from Kilkenny to the continent in peril of his life, in consequence of Popery again coming into power.

We have spoken of Archbishop Brown with somewhat reserved approval. We think it would have been better for himself, for the truth, for Dublin, and for Ireland, if he had possessed more moral courage; but we have intimated no doubt of his honest dissent from Rome. Ware transcribes a sermon which he, Brown, preached in Christ Church, perhaps on the day when the English liturgy was first used. Part of it has been thought somewhat prophetic of the course of the Jesuits, then just coming on the stage of Europe. His text was Psalm cxix. 18, "Open thou mine eyes, that I may behold wondrous things out of thy law." After applauding the translation of the Scriptures into the vulgar tongue, eulogizing the government, and exposing the folly and sin of worshipping and trusting images, he proceeds: "But there are a new fraternity of late sprung up, who call themselves Jesuits, which will deceive many, who are much after the Scribes' and Pharisees' manner amongst the Jews. They shall strive to abolish the truth, and shall come very near to do it; for these sorts will turn themselves into several forms: with the Heathen, an Heathenist; with Atheists, an Atheist; with the Jews, a Jew; and with the Reformers, a Reformade: purposely to know your intentions, your minds, your hearts, your inclinations, and thereby bring you at last to be like the fool that said in his heart there was no God. These shall spread over the whole world, shall be admitted to the councils of princes, and they never the wiser; charming of them, yea, making your princes reveal their hearts and the secrets therein unto them, and yet they not perceive it, which will happen from falling from the law of God, by neglect of fulfilling of the law of God, and by winking at their sins; yet, in the end, God, to justify his law, shall suddenly cut off this society, even by the hands of those who have most succored them and made use of them, so that at the end they shall become odious to all nations: they shall be worse than Jews, having no resting-place upon the earth, and then shall a Jew have more favor than a Jesuit." Brown could hardly have described the history of the Jesuits, during the latter half of the eighteenth century, more correctly, had he foreseen what then occurred in their expulsion from every Roman Catholic country in Europe, and the suppression of the order by a bull from Pope Ganganelli in 1773. But Brown's vision of the future seems not to have embraced the subsequent revival and reëstablishment of the brotherhood within the last fifty years, and the ascendency it is now seeking to acquire over the affairs of these countries, of Europe at large, and of America.

Mary, on coming to the throne in 1553, gave no token of resorting to those measure for exterminating Protestantism which not long afterwards struck terror into England's heart. The lords justices and privy council, in Dublin, issued a proclamation, making it lawful to attend the mass, but leaving all persons free to act as they chose in the matter. Afterwards, the Roman Catholic religion and the pope's supremacy were again established. Dowdal was recalled to Armagh and reinvested with the primacy. Brown of Dublin and four other prelates were removed from their sees, because they were married men. Bale, of Ossory, as before named, had to flee for his life. All the other bishops, however, were continued in their sees. Indeed, the whole affair passed off most quietly, so little hold had Protestant principles taken of the population. Persecution was scarcely heard of in Ireland, because there was little to persecute. This induced many of the English Protestants to cross over and reside where they would be free from the deadly violence to which they were exposed in their own land.

"Among others, John Hervey, Abel Ellis, John Edmonds, and Henry Hough, all Christian men, transported their effects to Dublin, and became citizens thereof; one Thomas Jones, a Welshman, and a Protestant priest, privately officiating among them." This was in 1554. But in a year or two the queen's government began to cast their eye upon the refugees, and an act " for reviving three [English] statutes, made for the punishment of heresies," was passed in a Dublin parliament. Perhaps it was deemed enough for the present to have these statutes held up *in terrorem*, for nothing appears to have been done towards putting them in force.

However, it would have been anomalous if Protestants had continued to enjoy life and liberty where popery was in strength. Within two months of the queen's death, namely, in October, 1558, the storm which had broken with desolating fury upon all that was dear to truth and godliness in England, began to move westward, and threatened to make havoc of the same in Ireland. Rarely has the historian had to record a more singular deliverance than in the case now referred to. It is, perhaps, generally known, but must not be omitted here. The reader shall have the account as given by Sir James Ware's son:

"Queen Mary, towards the end of her reign, this year granted a commission for to call the Protestants in question here in Ireland, as well as they had done in England; and to execute the same with greater force, she nominated Dr. Cole, sometime dean of St. Paul's in London, one of the commissioners; and so sent the commission by this said doctor. And in his journey coming to Chester, the mayor of that city, hearing that her majesty was sending commissioners into Ireland, and he being a churchman, waited on the doctor, who in his discourse with the mayor took out of his cloak-bag a leather box, and said unto him, 'Here is a commission that shall lash the heretics of Ireland,' calling the Protestants by that title. The good woman of the house being well affected to the Protestants and to that religion, and also having a brother, named John Edmonds, a Protestant and a citizen in Dublin, was much troubled at the Doctor's words. But she, waiting her convenient time, whilst the mayor took his leave of the doctor, and the doctor was complimenting him down the stairs, opened the box and took the commission out, and placed in lieu thereof a pack of cards, with the knave of clubs faced uppermost, and wrapt them up. The doctor coming up to his chamber, suspecting nothing of what had been done, put up his box as formerly. The next day, going to the water-side, wind and weather serving him, he sailed towards Ireland, and landed on the 17th of October, 1558, at Dublin. Then coming to the castle, the Lord Fitz-Walter being at this time lord deputy, sent for the doctor to come before him and the privy council, who coming in, after he had made a speech relating upon what account he came on, presented the box to the lord deputy, who causing it to be opened that the secretary might read the commission, there appeared nothing save a pack of cards, with the knave of clubs uppermost; which not only startled the lord deputy and the council, but the doctor, who assured them he had a commission, but knew not how it was gone. Then the lord deputy made answer, 'Let us have another commission, and we will shuffle the cards in the meanwhile.' The doctor, being troubled in his mind, went away, and returned into England, and coming to the court obtained another commission; but staying for a wind at the water-side, news came to him that the queen was dead. Thus," adds Ware, "God preserved the Protestants in Ireland from the persecution intended." As authorities for this extraordinary narrative, the writer of it mentions the Earl of Cork's "Memorials," Sir James Ware, and the two Primates Usher. He adds, that when Lord Fitz-Walter went to England after Elizabeth's accession, the deputy related the circumstances to her majesty, which so delighted the queen that she "sent for the good woman named Elizabeth Edmonds, by her husband Mattershed, and gave her a pension of forty pounds per annum *durante vitâ*, for saving her Protestant subjects of Ireland."

The new queen, Elizabeth, was proclaimed in Christ Church, Dublin, before the end of November, with the usual ceremonies. On the 27th of August following, Thomas, Earl of Sussex, landed at Dalkey, which seems to have been then a port of more importance than at present. He lay that night at Sir John Travers's house at Monktown. On the morrow, being Sunday, he came to Dublin, and was met by the mayor and aldermen on

Stephen's green, when he, the lord deputy, took the mayor by the hand, asked the aldermen how they did, and said, "You be all happy, my masters, in a gracious queen." That night he lay at one Mr. Peter Forth's house, because the house at Kilmainham, the usual residence of the deputy, once belonging to the Knights Templars, had been damaged by a great tempest the year before, and was not yet repaired. The next morning he rode to St. Patrick's, and then to St. Sepulchre's, where he kept his court. On the 30th he attended worship in Christ Church, where Sir Nicholas Darly sang the litany in English, after which the lord deputy took his oath of office. These ceremonies being ended, his lordship rode back to St. Sepulchre's, inviting the mayor and aldermen to dine with him. Soon after, the use of the mass-service was forbidden by proclamation. Orders came to the dean of Christ Church to remove from the cathedral all popish relics and images, and to paint and whiten it anew, putting sentences of Scripture upon the walls instead of pictures. This work was begun May 23d, 1559. In the same year the Archbishop of York sent over two large Bibles in English, one for each of the cathedrals, Christ Church and St. Patrick's. They were put up in the choir, and crowds of people flocked to see and read for themselves the sacred Scriptures of truth. So great was the demand thus created for Bibles, that John Dale, a Dublin bookseller, imported and sold for the London publishers not fewer than *seven thousand copies* in the two years ending with 1566.

The lord deputy having visited England to consult the court how he should manage respecting the affairs of the Church, returned in 1560, with instructions to call an assembly of the clergy, and to proceed with the establishment of the Protestant religion in Ireland. The convocation met. Some of the ecclesiastics were much angered, and one of them, William Walsh, bishop of Meath, having preached against the prayer-book, was, by the queen's commands, deposed and put in prison. By an act of parliament, the ecclesiastical jurisdiction was restored to the crown, and a new oath of supremacy appointed: the use of the common prayer was enforced, and all subjects were obliged to attend the service of the Church. English not being then the spoken language of the country, except in Dublin and a few other principal towns, it was ordered that where the people did not understand English, the service should be performed in *Latin!* The reason of this arrangement is not explained: possibly it may have been from a wish to meet the prejudices of Romanists, or from a fear of countenancing the Irish language, of which the English authorities seem generally to have had an instinctive dread.

Long before Elizabeth's time, great improvements had taken place in the house-building and general plan of Dublin. The structures of wattles plastered with clay had generally given place to those of "cage-work"—a framework of timber having the compartments filled up with brick or with wattles plastered, such as are yet to be seen in Chester and some other old English towns. Shingles, tiles, and slates, were taking the place of sedge and straw for roofing; although there were some thatched roofs in the city in the time of Charles I. One of the "cage" houses remained in Cooke street till about the middle of the last century: it was taken down on the 27th of July, 1745. "On an oak beam," says Whitelaw, "carried over the door the whole length of the said house, was the following inscription cut in large capitals and a fair Roman character, nothing damaged by time in the space of one hundred and sixty-five years, except in one part where an upright piece of timber, being morticed into it, had received the drip, and was somewhat rotted:—QUI FECISTI CŒLUM ET TERRAM BENEDIC DOMUM ISTAM, QUAM JOHANNES LUTREL ET JOHANA—NEI CONSTRUI FECERUNT, A. D. 1580, ET ANNO REGNI REGINÆ ELIZABETHÆ 22. 'Thou who madest the heavens and the earth bless this house, which John Lutrel and Joan—caused to be built in the year of our Lord 1580, and in the twenty-second year of the reign of Queen Elizabeth.'" Many other houses of the same sort were to be seen in the city and suburbs when this author wrote, namely, in 1766; but the one he considered to be the oldest and most remarkable was in Skinner's row, near the Tholsel: it had been called "the Cairbre," and was described as having been the residence of the lord-deputy Kildare, in 1532.

The "Tholsel," from *toll-stall*, or place where tolls were paid, above named as existing in 1766, was the successor of a previous one in Elizabeth's time, which also stood where now Nicholas street joins Christ Church Place, lately Skinner Row: it occupied the angle formed by the junction of the two, having its front towards the cathedral. "Newgate," the common jail, was a building of a square form, having a tower at each corner: it was one of the city gates, and stood in what was then called Newgate street, now Corn market, between New Row and High street. The Dublin "Bridewell" of Elizabeth's day was about halfway on the road from the city to where the college was built. The "Hospital" was on the river-side, near where Fleet street now is. The "Inns" of that time were followed in their site first by an "Infirmary," and then by the present "Four Courts."

The "Castle" was to have been built as a "palace" in addition to a fortress, but means had not been forthcoming for the purpose, and the representatives of the sovereign held their court at Thomas Court, or at St. Sepulchre's, the residence of the archbishop, or in the house of the Knights Templars at Kilmainham. Elizabeth, in the third year of her reign, 1560, commanded the lord lieutenant and council "to repair and enlarge the castle of Dublin, for the reception of the chief governors." The particulars of what was done in obedience to this order are not given us, but we are told that in 1567 the lord-deputy, Sir Henry Sidney, " repaired and beautified" it. Whatever the improvements were, they seem to have been neither adequate nor very durable, for within some seventy years afterwards it was in a ruinous condition, and Archbishop Laud wrote to the lord-deputy Wentworth to " vindicate to God's service" St. Andrew's *church*, which had been used by his lordship as a *stable*.

The " walls" of the city, in Elizabeth's reign, were in extent nearly as described in our last section, excepting that they now enclosed the space which then lay between them and the river. The principal streets within them were Castle street, Skinner Row, High street, Newgate street, St. Nicholas street, St. Werburgh's street, Back lane, Cooke street, Bridge street, Winetavern street, and Fish-shamble street. Merchant's Quay was the place where vessels landed their cargoes, and merchants carried on their business in imports and exports. Wood Quay, also, then existed. Between these two quays, at the foot of Winetavern street, stood the Custom House, called the " Crane." Beyond the walls on the south of the Liffey, were St. Andrew's, St. Michael-le-Pole's, St. Peter's, St. Stephen's, St. Bride's, and St. Catharine's churches, and St. Patrick's Cathedral ; with Thomas street, New Row, Francis street, Patrick street, Bride street, and Sheep street, more or less built, while indistinct rudiments showed themselves of the Coombe, New street, Kevin street, George's lane, and Dame street. A lodgment of water, called the City Ditch, ran from what is now Exchange court, to the foot of Nicholas street, having a bridge over it at Pole's gate, at the foot of Werburgh's street. The other gates were St. Nicholas's at the foot of St. Nicholas street, Newgate, Ormond gate, whence we now have "Wormwood" gate at the foot of New Row, Bridge gate opening from Bridge street to the Bridge, and Dame's gate leading into Dame street. The last was the principal entrance to the city, and was "armed" with a portcullis. As part of the city wall at the river end of Fish-shamble street, stood Finn's or rather Fynn's Castle, also called Proutefort's, a place of some strength, thought to have been built about the middle of the sixteenth century, and to have been named from its owner.

Parliament street and Essex street did not exist in Elizabeth's time: they, with Essex gate, were formed about 1672, when the Earl of Essex was lord lieutenant. Their place was, at the period we are describing, occupied by a creek, or small harbor for boats, which ran up from the river to near the head of Dame street. Here Archbishop Allen embarked when he fled from Fitzgerald in 1535, but, being driven on shore at Clontarf, he was discovered and put to death by the rebels. Along where we have Sycamore alley, Temple bar, Fleet street, and Poolbeg street, was covered with water at every rise of the tide. A village, called "Hoggins," occupied part of the space between George's lane and what is now Dawson street, probably about our Grafton street, and the village "Green" extended to the river: the name is thought to have come from the nunnery which stood there, " Ogh," in Irish signifying a " virgin." " Stephen's green" then existed, so called from the church of St. Stephen, which stood near it, but there was no road from it to Hoggin's green except through George's lane. Almost all the range beyond New Row, Thomas street, Francis street, Patrick's street, Sheep street, and Dame street, was considered " the country."

One bridge crossed the Liffey, namely, at the foot of Bridge street. There was also the " Ford" of St. Mary's Abbey, perhaps where Essex bridge has been since built. On the north side of the river were the Abbey and its lands, St. Michan's church, the Inns, and Ostmantown; with Churchstreet, Mary's lane, and Pill lane. The Liffey, more or less, flowed over what is Ormond Quay, Upper and Lower, and the adjoining parts.

" Good Queen Bess" made herself highly popular with the Dublin people, by the grant of three public clocks, which were put up, one at the Castle, a second at the Tholsel, and the other at St. Patrick's Cathedral. She also raised the value of the coin, so that the Dublin " shilling" passed for " nine-pence" in England.

A writer of this period tells us that " the hospitalitie of the maior and sherriffes for the year being is so large and bountifull, that surelie very few such officers under the crowne of England keep so great a port, none I am sure greater. The maior, over the number of officers that take their dailie repast at his table, keepeth for his yeare in a manner open house. And, albeit, in terme time his house is frequented as well of the nobilitie as of other potentates of great calling; yet his ordinarie is so good, that a verie few set feasts are provided for them. They that spend least in their maioraltie, (as those of credit, yea, and such as bare the office have informed me,) make an ordinarie account of five hundred pounds for their viand and diet that year: which is no small summe to be bestowed in housekeeping, namelie where vittels are so good cheape, and the presents of friends diverse and sundrie." It will, however, be seen that by the end of the queen's reign "vittels" had ceased to be "so good cheape," and that the chief magistrate's hospitalities must have declined, or that his expenditure thereon must have greatly increased.

We have now to record the establishment of the Dublin University, Elizabeth's great boon to Ireland.

It has been noticed that an institution of the kind was commenced, and existed for some time languishingly, at an earlier period, but at length died away. In 1568, a Dublin parliament projected another, to be supported by voluntary contributions; and the lord deputy, with other wealthy persons, promised liberal assistance. Representations were forwarded to London in order to obtain the sanction of the crown. Many delays and difficulties occurred to prevent this design from being carried into effect as quickly as it deserved. In 1590, it was renewed with greater vigor. St. Patrick's Cathedral had been occupied for the former university, and it was proposed to appropriate that edifice for the one now contemplated, but the archbishop, Loftus, would not give his consent, though zealous for the undertaking. However, accompanied by the lord chancellor and clergy, he met the mayor, aldermen, and commons, at the Tholsel, and after setting forth the advantages of having a seat of learning in the city, intimated that her majesty would be highly pleased if they would give the decayed monastery of All-Hallows, which Henry VIII., her father, had made over to the city, as a site for the erection. The mayor and corporation at once acquiesced. Applications for aid were made to the country, and from Cork, Galway, and other places, about £2000, equal to £14,000 now, was received towards the expenses of building, etc. The foundation-stone was laid by the mayor, on the 13th of March, 1591. The queen's charter of incorporation bears date March the 30th, 1592; and in January, 1593, the college was opened. It was based on liberal principles, much more so than is Oxford or even Cambridge, all Protestants, Conformists, or others, being eligible for its provostship and fellowships, as well as admissible to its advantages for education; but, in less than half a century from its beginning, Archbishop Laud greatly modified its constitution. Archbishop Loftus was the first provost, and the first three fellows were William Daniel and two Presbyterians from Scotland, who had been sent over by James VI. to watch his interests, and employed themselves as schoolmasters in the city. The first scholars, or students, were Abel Walsh, James

Usher, and James Lee. To some of the parties connected with the university in its earliest days, we must devote a few sentences.

The name best known among them is that of James Usher—a name that reflects honor upon his country and his age. He was born in Dublin on January the 8th, 1580: his father was one of the six clerks in chancery; his uncle, Henry Usher, was Archbishop of Armagh. The child James learned to read from two aunts who had been blind from their birth, but taught him the Bible from their recollection of it on its being read to them: he ever called it the "best of books." He was placed, for acquiring the elements of learning, under the care of Fullarton and Hamilton, the two Scottish schoolmasters, above referred to as made fellows of the college. James Usher entered college when only thirteen years old: Hamilton was his tutor there. In his nineteenth year, while yet a student, he accepted a challenge thrown out by Fitz-Symonds, a Jesuit, to a public disputation on the Protestant faith. The Jesuit reckoned on an easy triumph, but the stripling vanquished the giant. After a second conference, the latter declined a third. On this Usher wrote to him: the Jesuit sent no reply. He afterwards said of the discussion, "There came to me once a youth of about eighteen years of age, of a ripe wit, when scarce, as you would think, gone through his course of philosophy, or got out of his childhood, yet ready to dispute on the most abstruse points of divinity." The same Jesuit called Usher "*Acatholicorum doctissimus*"—the "most learned

THE BRITISH REFORMATION. 85

of the not-Catholics." In 1601, he was ordained by his uncle, the primate, and preached a series of controversial sermons in Christ Church with great success. What he afterwards became is known to the world.

William Daniel, one of the first fellows of the university, was the first or second who took there the degree of doctor in divinity. He was consecrated Archbishop of Tuam in 1609. He was an eminent scholar, and translated the New Testament out of Greek into the Irish language; which work was printed in quarto, and dedicated to King James I. It was reprinted in 1681, at the expense of the Honorable Robert Boyle. Daniel also translated the English Common Prayer into Irish. This was printed in 1608, and dedicated to the lord deputy, Sir Arthur Chichester.

Archbishop Loftus took the honorary title of "provost" to the college at its opening, in order to countenance the undertaking, but shortly resigned the office, and arranged that Walter Travers, a Puritan, who had been joint-fellow with himself in Trinity College, Cambridge, should succeed him. Travers was afternoon preacher at the Temple church, London, where Hooker, author of the Ecclesiastical Polity, preached in the morning. The two ministers were strongly at variance on doctrinal and ecclesiastical matters: the same pulpit, in one part of the day, was antagonist to itself in the other. Hooker took deep umbrage, and failing to carry the mind of the congregation with him, appealed to a higher authority, Whitgift, the Archbishop of Canterbury, who, says Thomas Fuller in his Church History, "silenced Travers from preaching in the Temple or anywhere else. It was laid to his charge :—1. That he was no lawful ordained minister of the Church of England. 2. That he preached here without license. 3. That he had broken the order made in the seventh year of her majesty's reign, that erroneous doctrine, if it came to be publicly taught, should not be publicly refuted, but that notice thereof should be given to the ordinary, to hear and determine such causes, to prevent public disturbance." Hearing of what had thus occurred in London, Loftus wrote to Travers, inviting him to the provostship of the Dublin college. Travers acceded, and remained in that office till ill-health obliged him to resign in 1601, when he returned to England. Fuller gives him the highest character. "Sometimes," he writes, "he did preach; rather when he dared than when he would: debarred from all cure of souls for his nonconformity." Usher, who had studied under him, held him in high veneration, and, when Travers was in poverty for conscience' sake, offered him money; but Travers " returned a thankful refusal thereof." He "bequeathed all his books of oriental languages, (wherein he was exquisite,) and plate worth fifty pounds, to Sion College in London. O! if this good man had had a hand to his head, or rather a purse to his hand, what charitable works would he have left behind him! But," continues Fuller, in concluding a pretty full account of him, "in pursuance of his memory, I have entrenched too much on the modern times. Only this I will add, perchance the reader will be angry with me for saying thus much; and I am almost angry with myself for saying no more of so worthy a divine."

The University, in its charter of incorporation, was styled *Collegium Sanctæ et Individuæ Trinitatis Juxta Dublin à Serenissimâ Reginâ Elizabethâ Fundatum.* The "Juxta" is inappropriate to describe its position now, its situation being in one of the greatest thoroughfares of the city. Its first buildings formed a square, the principal of them being on the north side. Within a few years of its commencement, its revenues failed in consequence of a rebellion in the country, and applications had to be made to the government for funds to prevent its being finally closed. The necessary aid was granted, and this university is at present second to neither Oxford nor Cambridge in the ability and zeal of its professors, its general regulations, or the conduct of the resident students. But "Trinity," in its beginning, had a very humble form compared with the noble establishment of our own day, including its handsome frontage, its magnificent library and its chapel, its examination-hall, its dining-hall, its printing-office, its squares, its spacious park for recreation, its botanic garden on the east, and its observatory on the west of the metropolis it adorns.

The rebellion which imperilled the infant college was only one of a succession which kept the country in ferment to nearly the close of Elizabeth's reign, when the English power came to be generally acknowledged. Of the distress occasioned by these wars, some opinion may be formed by the following account of the prices at which provisions were sold in Dublin in the year 1602, signed by John Tirrel, the mayor. Wheat had risen from 36s. the quarter to 180s.; barley-malt from 10s. the barrel to 43s.; oatmeal from 5s. the barrel to 22s.; peas from 5s. the peck to 40s.; oats from 3s. 4d. the barrel to 20s.; beef from 26s. 8d. the carcase to £8; mutton from 3s. the carcase to 26s.; veal from 10s. the carcase to 29s.; a lamb from 1s. to 6s.; a pork from 8s. to 30s. If we multiply these prices by *seven*, to give their equivalents in our own money, the sums almost exceed belief, and show that if money were not in proportion much more plentiful than it is with us, the cost of what are considered necessaries must at that period have been, with most persons, tantamount to a prohibition of them.

SECTION IV.

DUBLIN UNDER JAMES I. AND CHARLES I.

Allusion has already been made to the frequent occurrence of pestilence in Dublin. In the year 1575, a plague broke out on the 7th of June, and continued till the 17th of October, carrying off at least three thousand persons. The city is described as having been then so depopulated, by deaths or desertions, that grass grew in the streets and about the church-doors. The mayor and sheriffs held their court at Glasmanogue, and the lord deputy resided at Drogheda. In 1604, the same calamity began in October and continued till September, 1605. It broke out again the next year, and continued till the year following. Yet the annals record that in the year 1610 the inhabitants of the city and suburbs amounted to twenty thousand. The density with which the people were crowded together, the want of sewerage, and, equally, of cleanliness and ventilation, with the malaria from the swamps bordering on the river and elsewhere near the city, must have almost compelled disease in some of its worst forms to hold the place as its den and throne.

Notwithstanding all that Elizabeth's government had done to make Ireland Protestant, little, very little, had been effected. The poet Spenser gives an appalling account of what he had observed to be the state of both clergy and laity in the country, and he places in humiliating contrast the earnestness of the Roman priesthood and the supineness and selfishness of what he calls "the ministers of the gospel."

Lord Bacon thought much for Ireland, and in 1601 wrote to Cecil, secretary of state, urging "some course of advancing religion indeed, where the people is capable thereof; as the sending over some good preachers, especially of that sort which are vehement and zealous preachers, and not scholastic, to be resident in principal towns, endowing them with some stipend out of her majesty's revenues, as her majesty hath most religiously and graciously done in Lancashire; and the re-continuing and replenishing the college begun in Dublin, the placing of good men to be bishops in the sees there, and the taking care of the versions of Bibles, and catechisms, and other books of instruction in the Irish language; and the like religious courses, both for the honor of God, and for the avoiding of scandal and unsatisfaction here, by the show of toleration in religion in some parts there." Little or no notice appears to have been taken of Bacon's advice.

It may be hoped that Dublin itself was not so destitute of faithful Christian ministrations in the beginning of the seventeenth century as Spenser's statements show too many portions of the island to have been. Travers, who remained provost of the college till 1601, must have had some influence for the truth of the gospel in the city. Usher, also, had been catechist-reader in the college, and, about 1602, was appointed afternoon preacher in Christ Church, where the court attended.

Having mentioned Usher's connection with the college, we may add that the English army, when they had defeated the Spaniards and disaffected Irish in the south of the country, raised among themselves the sum of £1800 to furnish a library for the Dublin University, and placed it in the hands of "Dr. Challoner and Mr. James Usher," to be expended in the purchase of books for the purpose. The military have seldom perhaps been thus forward in such good works; but, as we shall see, this was not the last instance of the college library deriving aid from the bountifulness of the English soldiery.

Under the date of 1605, Whitelaw's "History of Dublin" records, "The Jesuits and seminary priests busied themselves greatly in dissuading the people from resorting to Divine service according to the Act of Uniformity, and the king's proclamation thereon grounded. The lord deputy (Chichester) and council convened before them the aldermen and some of the principal citizens, and endeavored by persuasions and lenity to draw them to their duty. They also exemplified under the great seal, and published the Statute of Uniformity of the 2d of Elizabeth, in regard there was found to be some material difference between the original record and the printed copies, that none might pretend ignorance of the original record, and added thereto the king's injunction for the observance of the said statute. But these gentle methods failing to have any effect, sixteen of the most eminent men of the city were convened into the court of the "Castle Chamber"—answering to the "Star Chamber" in England—"of whom nine of the chief were censured, and six of the aldermen fined each £100, and the other three £50 a-piece; and they were all committed prisoners to the Castle during the pleasure of the court; and it was ordered that none of the citizens should bear office till they conformed. The week following, the rest were censured in the same manner, except alderman Archer, who conformed. Their fines were allotted to the repairs of such churches as had been damaged by an accidental blowing up of gunpowder in 1596, to the relieving poor scholars in the college, and other charitable uses. This proceeding brought many to an outward conformity." The "blowing up of the gunpowder" mentioned, was an explosion of 144 barrels which had been landed at Wood Quay, and stored in Winetavern street for the use of the Castle. Nearly fifty houses were burned, and about four hundred lives lost by this accident.

The measures adopted to enforce Protestantism, provoked resistance to the government on the part of the Romanists. In 1607, a conspiracy was formed between the Earls of Tyrone and Tyrconnel, with other leading persons, to seize the castle, cut off the lord deputy and the council, dissolve the state, and set up a new authority. A Roman Catholic who had been invited to join, but who shrank from the design, dropped a letter in the Council Chamber, addressed to Sir William Usher, clerk of the council, giving the particulars of the plan as they had been made known to him. The conspirators were apprised that they had been betrayed, and fled before they could be apprehended; but their estates were confiscated.

After an interval of twenty-seven years, a parliament was once more called in 1613. The two parties disagreed on the choice of a speaker, and the Romanists withdrew. Another met the year after; and a convocation of the clergy was held which adopted a code of "articles" as the Confession of the Irish Church. This formulary of faith was prepared by Usher: it was essentially Puritanic, being rigidly Calvinistic in doctrine, and liberal in matters ritual and eccesiastical. It declared the pope to be the Man of Sin; taught that Lent is of merely political, not religious obligation; and affirmed that the Lord's-day is to be *wholly* devoted to the service of God. It set forth that the catholic or invisible Church includes all the faithful on earth and in heaven; but that "particular and visible Churches (consisting of those who make profession of the faith of Christ, and live under the outward means of salvation) be many in number; wherein the more or less sincerely according to Christ's institution, the word of God is taught, the sacraments are duly administered, and the authority of the keys is used, the more or less pure are such churches to be accounted." It makes no reference to the consecration of prelates, as if, in Collyer's judgment, done on purpose to avoid the distinction between the episcopal order and that of presbyters; and Neal thinks it was "contrived to compromise the difference between the Church and the Puritans:" which effect, he says, it had till 1634, when, by the influence of Archbishop Laud and the Earl of Strafford, these articles were set aside, and others received in their stead. It was feared that Usher would incur the king's displeasure by the tenor of these articles, and attempts were not wanting to prejudice James against him for the leading part he took in the adoption of a confession by the Irish Church, which included much that was contrary to the king's principles. "But Usher," writes Leland, "had the address to guard against the insinuations of his enemies; and James was so just to his piety and erudition, that he soon after promoted him to the see of Meath."

A notice of the neighborhood of Dublin about this period occurs incidentally in an account of the state of Ulster, given when James was parcelling out six counties of it which were at his disposal in consequence of confiscations. "Sir Toby Caufield's people are driven every night to lay up all his cattle, as it were in ward; and do he and his what they can, the woolfe and the wood-kernae"—a marauder living in the wood—"within culiver shot of his fort, have oftentimes a share." "Even in the English pale," he adds, "Sir John King and Sir Henry Harrington, within half a mile of Dublin, do the like, for these forenamed enemies do every night survey the fields to the very walls of Dublin."

A proclamation for banishing the Roman Catholic regular clergy was issued in October, 1617. But, in five years afterwards, that party opened a university in Back Lane, for the education of persons of their own persuasion: Whitelaw, indeed, dates this establishment later. When Lord Falkland came over as lord deputy, Usher preached before him in Christ Church, and the Roman Catholics took umbrage at the sermon as intended to encourage persecution against them: to satisfy them, he delivered an explanatory discourse, which, however, it is likely did not give them the satisfaction desired. In November following, "several popish magistrates, who had refused the oath of supremacy, contrary to the statute of 2 Eliz. cap. 1, were censured in the Star Chamber, when Bishop Usher made a speech about the lawfulness of the oath." And, in two months more, there was "issued a proclamation requiring the popish clergy, regular and secular, to depart the kingdom within forty days, and forbidding all intercourse with them after that time."

Notwithstanding all that could be done to suppress them, the lord deputy found himself unable to keep the disaffected in check. They were aware that the revenue of the country fell seriously short of the expenditure, and that the authorities had not power at command to control them. The troubled state of England on Charles's accession and assumption of arbitrary power, gave yet more confidence to the Romanist hierarchy and laity. They judged it a favorable juncture for obtaining a toleration for their religion; and it was not for Charles, in his circumstances, to slight the applications of a party so important. Its leaders were admitted to a conference on the subject with the authorities in Dublin. They intimated that for a partial toleration they would give a voluntary contribution for supporting the army. "A grand meeting of the principal nobility and gentry, in which the popish party was by far the more numerous, assembled in the Castle of Dublin: they offered large contributions to purchase security to their lands and a suspension of the penal statutes. Lord Falkland, far from discouraging their overtures, advised them to send agents to England, to make a tender of their dutiful services to the king, and to submit the grievances and inconveniences to which they were exposed, to his gracious consideration." These movements alarmed the Protestants. Usher and eleven other prelates met in Dublin, and entered a strong protest against the measure. This protest was read from the Dublin pulpits, and Usher was requested to explain the grounds of it in a speech before the council for the conviction of the parties it concerned; and his address, though it failed of its purpose, was considered worthy of being sent over to the king, who highly approved of it.

The Irish agents, however, were successful at the English court. It was greatly in their favor that money and strength were at the time of greater value to Charles, if they were not always nearer to his heart, than Protestant orthodoxy. They offered his majesty a hundred and twenty thousand pounds, payable in quarterly instalments, on condition of receiving in return certain royal "graces," which were to be affirmed by parliament. Several of these "graces," it is to be observed, affected the property and trade of the country, and were by all parties reckoned just and beneficial. Respecting ecclesiastical matters, it was agreed that bishops and patentees of dissolved monasteries should be equally subject to the state burdens with other persons; and, "as the popish recusants had clamored against the severe demands of the established clergy, it was provided that all unlawful exactions taken by the clergy be reformed and regulated; and the rigor," writes Leland, "with which their (the clergy's) demands had been enforced, may be gathered from the injunction annexed: 'That no extraordinary warrants of assistance, touching clandestine marriages, christenings, or burials, or any contumacies pretended against ecclesiastical jurisdiction, are to be issued or executed by any chief governor; nor are the clergy to be permitted to keep any private prisons of their own for these causes, but delinquents in that kind are henceforth to be committed to the king's public jails and by the king's officers.'"

The success of the Irish deputies with Charles well nigh intoxicated the "recusants," as the Roman Catholics were now called. Their worship was openly celebrated in due form and with great pomp. Parochial churches were seized for their service. Their ecclesiastical jurisdiction was strictly administered. New friaries and nunneries were erected. Priests from foreign seminaries swarmed into the country and its metropolis, sworn to hatred against England and to allegiance to the pope, under the direction of the *Propagandâ Fide*, then lately established. These swellings of Romanism stirred the fears and the zeal of Protestants. Accustomed to look to the government as their stay, instead of being themselves valiant for the truth in the use of truth's own weapons, and relying upon God whose the truth and its triumphs are, they obtained a proclamation from the government, forbidding the exercise of the Roman Catholic worship. The Roman Catholics despised the proclamation, and became yet more bold, conscious of their superiority in the kind of strength on which Protestantism was then made to rest as its safeguard. They complained that their agents in England had exceeded their powers in engaging so large a contribution to the king, and that the country was not able to bear the impost. Falkland was recalled, and Viscount Ely, the lord chancellor, and the Earl of Cork, lord high treasurer, were sworn lords justices. They proceeded forthwith to execute the laws against " recusants," and to compel attendance on the established worship. But intimation came that such measures were not pleasing to the king. The Romanists were in consequence cheered on. A fraternity of Carmelites appeared in public, wearing the habit of their order, and celebrated their worship in one of the most frequented parts of the city. This was not to be endured. The archbishop and the mayor led a body of troops to their chapel, to disperse the congregation. The congregation, headed by the priests, repelled the assailants: the archbishop, the mayor, and the military, had to save themselves by flight. An order now came from London for the seizure of sixteen religious houses for the king's use, and for the transfer of the Roman Catholic College to the Dublin University.

Affairs were in this position when Wentworth, afterwards Earl of Strafford, arrived as lord deputy in July, 1633. He came, resolved to break down all power in the country, Romanist or Protestant, to the king's will as absolute and universal law. Wentworth brought with him Dr. Bramhall, afterwards Bishop of Derry, a man sufficiently endowed with abilities and erudition, but whose ideas of doctrine and discipline were so consonant with those of Laud, that Oliver Cromwell afterwards called him the "Canterbury of Ireland."

A new influence was now brought to bear upon the Irish Established Church. Some of its first measures had reference to altering the place of the communion tables in the castle chapel and Christ Church cathedral, and ordering the Earl of Cork to take down a family monument lately erected at the east end of the choir in St. Patrick's. But its most important work was changing the Church's profession of faith. The Puritanic cast of the Irish Church greatly encouraged the anti-Laud party in England. "If, therefore," writes Heylin, in his Life of Laud, "the archbishop meant to have peace in England, the Church of Ireland must be won to desert those articles, and receive ours in England in the place thereof." Heylin's description of the *management* by which the change was brought about, shows Jesuitism of a high order, and proves that the majority of the Irish clergy, with Usher at their head, in convocation at Dublin, were beguiled to adopt resolves contrary alike to their intentions and convictions. "Usher and his party," says Heylin, "found, too late, that by receiving and approving the English Articles, they had abrogated and repealed the Irish." "To salve this sore," Usher and some bishops of his opinion, at the next ordinations, required subscriptions to the Articles of both churches, which, however, was not required afterwards, through the inconsistency it involved. Usher next applied to the lord deputy to have the former Irish confession ratified anew by parliament; but the lord deputy threatened to have that confession burned by the common hangman; and, when nothing availed on the Irish side of the channel, assurances were sent to persons of distinction in England that the Irish Articles were not recalled. "But all this," Heylin somewhat exultingly records, "would not serve the turn, or save those articles from being brought under repeal by the present canon." He intimates, that the abrogation of the Irish Articles which asserted the sanctity of the Lord's Day, removed an objection to his majesty's declaration about lawful sports on that day; and he quotes from Fuller, that "the Irish Articles, wherein Arminianism was condemned in *terminis terminantibus*, and the observation of the Lord's Day resolved *Jure Divino*, were utterly excluded."

Thus Laud triumphed over the Irish Church. The Dublin college was regulated with comparative ease. He was appointed its chancellor, and remodelled its constitution and statutes, so far as policy would allow, after his own mind. To make Laud's victory doubly sure, a court of High Commission was established in Dublin: a fit coadjutor to the court of Castle Chamber, or Irish Star Chamber, already existing.

From affairs ecclesiastical, arranged so ably for Laud by Bramhall, we now turn to affairs secular, not quite so well adjusted for Charles by Wentworth. In the parliament which sat during the convocation in 1634, the lord deputy obtained in the commons a vote of six subsidies, amounting in the whole to *two hundred and forty thousand pounds:* the vote was encumbered only with *recommendations* as to the modes in which the money should be applied. The lords were not quite so accommodating. They required a redress of "grievances" and a confirmation of the "graces," particularly the one which limited the king's title to lands. Against their resolve Wentworth entered a protest, founded on an act called, from its author, Poyning's, which required that no bill should be proposed in the Irish parliament that had not been approved by the king in council.

An apparently trifling incident, but one which was really important, happened in the beginning of this parliament. To prevent danger from collisions of opinion which might arise in the heat of debate, an order had once been given that peers, on entering the house, should leave their swords with the usher of the black rod. Wentworth revived this order. The young Earl of Ormond presented himself at the door, but refused to comply with the usher's demand. The official insisted on his submission. Ormond replied, that if he must receive his sword it should be in his body; and, not waiting for permission, entered the house and took his seat. The lord deputy, highly incensed, summoned Ormond to answer for his conduct. "The young lord appeared, avowed his knowledge of the order, and his own wilful disobedience; but added, that he had received the investiture of his earldom *per cincturam gladii*, and was both entitled and bound by the royal command to attend his duty in parliament *gladio cinctus*. Wentworth," continues Leland, "was abashed and confounded. He consulted his friends whether he should at once crush or reconcile this daring spirit. They reminded him of the necessity of gaining some of the great personages of Ireland: of the power, connections, and capacity of the earl: of the good disposition he had already discovered to the interests of the crown, and of his influence in the house of peers." These considerations weighed with Wentworth to attempt reconciling the refractory Ormond, who soon became a particular favorite at the Irish court, and at the age of twenty-four had a seat in the privy council. Winning Ormond over to the king's party was a gain to Charles in Ireland, hardly second in value to Charles's alienating Wentworth from the popular side in England and attaching him to the royal cause.

"The splendor of the court of Dublin during the vice-royalty of Strafford," observes the Irish Quarterly Review, "far exceeded any thing before known in the city. 'Other deputies,' says the earl, in 1633, 'kept never a horse in their stables, put up the king's pay for their troop and company in a manner clear into their purses, infinitely to his majesty's disservice, in the example: I have threescore good horses in mine, which will stand me in twelve hundred pounds a year, and a guard of fifty men waiting on his majesty's deputy every Sunday, personable men and well appointed. Other deputies have kept their tables for thirty pounds a week: it stands me (besides my stable) in three score and ten pounds when it is at least.' The author of the *Epistolæ Ho-Elianæ*, writing from Dublin during Strafford's vicegerency, says, 'Here is a most splendid court kept at the castle, and except that of the viceroy of Naples, I have not seen the like in Christendom; and in one point of grandeza the lord deputy here goes beyond him, for he can confer honors and dub knights, which that viceroy cannot, or any other that I know of. Traffick increaseth here wonderfully, with all kinds of bravery and buildings.' A tourist, who had travelled through Holland, the United Provinces, England, and Scotland, tells us, in 1635, that 'Dublin is, beyond all exception, the fairest, richest, best built city he had met with, (except York and Newcastle :) it is far beyond Edinborough: only one street in Edinborough (the great long street) surpasseth any street here. Here is the lord deputy, and the state and council of the kingdom.' 'This city of Dublin,' continues the same author, 'is extending his bounds and limits very far: much additions of building lately, and some of them very fine, stately, and complete buildings: every commodity is grown very dear. You must pay also for an horse hire 1s. 6d. a day. There are various commodities cried in Dublin as in London, which it doth more resemble than any other town I have seen in the King of England's dominions.'"

"The excess to which luxury in dress was carried in Dublin about this period, called forth the interference of the legislature, and in 1634 it was ordered by the Irish house of commons, that 'the proposition made against the excessive wearing of bone lace, and of gold and silver lace, should be referred to the consideration of the committee of grievances, to consider what persons and degrees are fit to use the same, and how, for to report their opinion thereon to the house.'"

Not fewer than fifty peers attended the parliament called by Wentworth, and they, with the members of the lower house, must have added much to the trade and splendor of the city. Some families of distinction had mansions worthy of their rank. Among them was the Earl of Cork's, at the Dame's gate, near the castle, from which the ascent there acquired the name of "Cork Hill." This building was afterwards taken on lease by the government of Charles I., and it was occupied for public purposes early under the commonwealth, though by that time it had fallen much into decay.

Little, it is to be feared, can be said favorable to the state of Christian piety in Dublin at this period. Dr. Joshua Hoyle occupied the pulpit of St. Werburgh's, where he is said to have preached at ten in the morning and at three in the afternoon. He is described as "the friend of Usher, and the tutor and chamber-fellow of Sir James Ware," "a most zealous preacher and general scholar in all manner of learning." He was a fellow and professor of divinity in the university. He appeared as one of the witnesses against Laud on his trial, and afterwards was a constantly-attending member of the Westminster Assembly of Divines. Wood, in the "Athenæ Oxonienses," gives him a high character. He had studied at Oxford, and died master of University College there in 1654.

Notwithstanding all the gayety and appearance of prosperity in the metropolis, the elements of strife already adverted to were generating fearful convulsions in the country. Rome, by its bulls, its nuncio, its emissaries, conspired with Charles's self-seeking tyranny and duplicity, to sever it from England and Protestantism together; but the details of organizations and movements directed to this end belong to the history of Ireland rather than of Dublin. The lord deputy's rule here was of the same tenor with that of his master: it aggravated discontent in the honest and well-disposed, while it cheered on the revolted. Wentworth returned to England, where he was created Earl of Strafford. He was impeached, attainted, and executed. Sir Christopher Wandsford was appointed lord deputy, but died suddenly. Sir William Parsons and Sir John Borlase were sworn lords justices in February, 1641. The insurgents had their schemes laid widely, but with so much secrecy that the authorities were totally unaware of their intentions. They had prepared to possess themselves of Dublin, with its castle, and on the 22nd of October they resolved to effect their purpose on the evening of the next day.

Providentially for the city, its inhabitants, and the government, one Mac Mahon, a leader among the rebels, had disclosed their projects to a man named Owen O'Connolly, servant to a Protestant gentleman in the north, hoping to engage him with them. This man came up to Dublin in quest of a friend on the 22d, when he met Mac Mahon, and while they were drinking together, the latter divulged to him the plan for the following day. Half-intoxicated as he was, O'Connolly stole away and gave information to Sir William Parsons. The man's appearance made Sir William for the moment pay little regard to his statements. He was told to go and obtain further information. But he was hardly dismissed when it struck Sir William that what the man had said was more important than it at first seemed to be. He ordered the castle and city to be guarded, and went to his fellow lord justice, Sir John Borlase. The privy council were summoned. Messengers were sent to discover and bring O'Connolly again. He was found with the police, who had taken him in charge for not being able to give an account of himself. By his disclosures, Mac Mahon, Lord Maguire, and some more, were arrested; but other leaders, hearing of the discovery, saved themselves by instant flight. Most opportunely, Sir Francis Willoughby, governor of Galway Castle, a privy-councillor and an able soldier, reached Dublin at this critical moment. He found the gates closed and the suburbs in much confusion. Hearing that the lords justices and the privy council were in deliberation at Sir John Borlase's, on the green leading to the college, he went thither. He told them that in the country through which he passed he observed no signs of disturbance, but that an unusual number of strange horsemen had all night been pouring into the suburbs. He recommended an adjournment to the castle for greater security. The lords justices and council acted on his suggestions, assigned to him the general defence of the place, and issued a proclamation informing the public of the plot discovered, and exhorting to loyalty and courage in self-defence.

The force at the command of the government did not exceed three thousand men, and these were scattered in garrisons and detachments through the country. In Dublin castle were " one thousand five hundred barrels of powder, with proportionate match and bullet, arms for ten thousand men, and thirty-five pieces of artillery with all their equipage." For its security were "eight infirm wardens and forty halberdiers," being the parade guard of the chief magistrate on state occasions. Willoughby was prompt and energetic. "The council table was his only couch. He could not venture to lay down his drawbridge without the attendance of his whole insignificant guard, until the arrival of a part of his disbanded regiment from Carlisle enabled him to arm two hundred men for the defence of the castle; a body soon reinforced by those who fled for shelter to the capital, and by some detachments of the army recalled from their quarters by the lords justices."

Nothing could exceed the consternation of the citizens. Rumors the most appalling flew like lightning. Many of the English went on board vessels in the river to return to their native country, and, though wind-bound, preferred remaining on the water to venturing on land again. A fleet of Scotch fishermen offered five hundred of their men for the service of the state, but just as the offer was accepted, they set sail under a false alarm. Four hundred soldiers, embarked for the service of Spain, and detained by order of the English parliament, were not permitted to leave the ships till they were nearly perishing from hunger, and eventually they dispersed to join the rebel cause. However, under the advice of Sir John Temple, Master of the Rolls, the principal Protestant merchants of the city deposited their goods and valuables in the castle, under a guarantee of payment for whatever should be applied to the public service. Thus provisions were obtained when the treasury was exhausted, and when the magistrates of the city could not or would not advance money to the government.

Dublin was saved and became tranquil. Not so the country. In the course of the ensuing winter, horrors were perpetrated the accounts of which make the blood run cold as we read them in our own day. "Forty thousand persons, and by some computations," writes Godwin, "five times that number, are said to have perished in this undistinguishing massacre."

Charles, unable to adjust matters with the Parliament, appealed to arms in support of his prerogative. In August, 1642, he unfurled his standard at Nottingham. "A high wind beat down the flag, an evil omen, as it was deemed by some who saw it, and a symbol as it proved of the result of that unnatural conflict." At length, Ireland became the *dernier resort* of the royal cause. Ormond was made lord deputy and commander of the army. He soon found himself in a position of difficulty between two antagonists— the friends of Protestantism, and the Roman Catholic confederates — neither of whom now cared much for his sovereign, but against both of whom, though hostile the one to the other, he felt it impossible to maintain his ground. The month of February, 1647, found him yet in Dublin, but under the necessity of deciding to which party he would yield. His choice was in favor of the English parliament. In April, several of their regiments arrived, and in June came their commissioners with more troops. To these Ormond formally surrendered Dublin, Drogheda, then called Tredagh, and other garrisons; and in July he delivered up into their hands the insignia of his authority, and went to England. One of the three persons given by Ormond as hostages for this capitulation, was the eminent Sir James Ward, "the Camden of Ireland."

Thus ended the reign of Charles over Dublin. The city was in a most wretched and dilapidated state. By returns dated August, 1644, its inhabitants numbered—Protestants, 2,565 men, and 2,986 women; Roman Catholics, 1,202 men, and 1,406 women; total, 8,159. But perhaps this census embraced only adults; or, which is more probable, it did not include the suburbs; otherwise the population had decreased three-fifths during the preceding thirty-four years—a diminution incredible, even with every allowance for havoc made by war, pestilence, and famine.

SECTION V.

DUBLIN AT THE COMMONWEALTH, THE RESTORATION, AND THE REVOLUTION.

On the surrender of Dublin to the parliamentary commissioners, they appointed colonel Michael Jones to be its governor with the command of the troops. His first care was to repair the walls and otherwise to prepare the city for defence against the army of the confederates which threatened it. Within a fortnight after Ormond had left, Jones marched forth and attacked them at Duggan's Hill, gaining a complete victory. They are said to have had between five and six thousand slain in the engagement; fifteen of their field-officers, and eighty-four other commissioned officers were among the prisoners; while Jones lost only twenty men. Besides artillery and other spoil, sixty-four "fair oxen" fell into his hands, and proved a most seasonable supply. A person giving an account of the battle, wrote, "All their colors we have, which Colonel Jones would not be persuaded to have brought into Dublin with triumph, as savoring (said he) of ostentation, and attributing to man the glory of this great work due to the Lord alone." By November, however, the rebel leader, Owen Roe O'Neil, was committing such devastations in the neighborhood of Dublin, that not fewer than two hundred fires were visible at the same time from one of the church steeples.

Ormond, still attached to Charles, and thinking it possible even yet to retrieve his royal master's affairs, returned to Ireland. In January, 1648-9, he concluded a peace with the confederates, in the king's name and behalf. Charles, or Glamorgan, whom he accredited for the purpose, had often negotiated and made peace with them before, and as often had the terms agreed on been disallowed or broken through. Lord Inchiquin also now made common cause with the Irish: the Scots of Ulster, too, ranged themselves against the parliament and the "sectaries." Early in 1649, Oliver Cromwell was appointed by the parliament their lord-lieutenant for Ireland. He invited the eminent Dr. John Owen, whose "Exposition of the Hebrews" and other works, are yet well known and valued, to accompany him as chaplain, and to regulate the affairs of Trinity College. To this, after much difficulty, Owen acceded. The army for Ireland, under Cromwell's command, assembled at Milford Haven in August, and the day before embarking was spent by them in fasting and prayer.

About this juncture, Dublin was in deep distress. Jones, its governor, was closely pressed by Ormond and the confederates, who had encamped at Finglass, but on July the 25th had removed to Rathmines, on the opposite side of the city. There Jones attacked them with success. The parliament ordered his dispatch to be printed for the information of the English public. Some extracts from this small old pamphlet may interest the reader. The battle is sometimes mentioned as fought at "Bagotrath," a place between Donnybrook and Beggar's Bush, now occupied by Upper Bagot street, taking its name from a "rath" or fort there, which, in the thirteenth century, came into the possession of the "Bagot" family. The conflict probably waxed strongest over the lands extending from that place to Rathmines. Rathmines was then "compassed by a wall about sixteen feet high, and inclosing ten acres of ground."

The pamphlet has for its title—"Lieutenant-General Jones's Letter to the Council of State, of a Great Victory which it had pleased God to give the forces, in the City of Dublin, under his command on the Second of this instant August, against the Earl of Ormond's and the Lord Inchiquin's forces before the City." Jones's letter begins: "Right Honorable: the Lord hath blessed this your army with good success against Ormond and his, for which God's most holy name be glorified." After giving the particulars of the engagement, he proceeds: "The whole work is the Lord's doing, and it is marvellous in our eyes: by whose especial providence it was that we should thus engage, we ourselves at first not so far intending it; neither did the enemy expect our doing so; nor would they have willingly engaged with us, if it might have been by them avoided, they reserving themselves for the coming up of Clanricard with his Connaught forces, about three thousand, and the Lord of Ard's with his seven thousand Scots, all ready for marching; Inchiquin also being looked for, who had the week before gone towards Munster, with two regiments of horse, for appeasing some stirrings there by Owen Roe, raised in his absence. Never was any day in Ireland like this, to the confusion of the Irish, and to the raising up of the spirits of the poor English, and to the restoring of the English interest, which, from their first footing in Ireland, was never in so low a condition as at that very instant, there not being one considerable landing-place left you but this alone, and this also (without this the Lord's most gracious goodness and providence to us) almost gone," etc. "Your honor's most faithful servant, Mic. Jones. Dated Dublin, Aug. 6, 1649." In addition to the numbers slain, Jones took prisoners seventeen field officers, and more than 150 other commissioned officers. Of the troops taken, 1,500 joined the parliamentary service. "A list of artillery taken from the Irish at Ramines, the 2d of August, 1649. One brass cannon, weighing 7,321 pounds, her length 10 feet, her bullet weighing 44 pounds. One brass demi-cannon eldest, weighing 5,428 pounds, her length 11½ feet, her bullet weighing 32 pounds. Two brass demi-cannon of one mould, each weighing 4,400 pounds, their length 9½ feet, their bullet weighing 26 pounds. One square brass demi-culverin weighing 2,800 pounds, her length 11 feet 4 inches, her bullet weighing 12 pounds. One small brass saker-drake, weighing 600 pounds, her length 4½ feet, her bullet weighing 6 pounds. One brass mortar-piece weighing 927 pounds, her shell weighing 100 pounds." "Captain Otway, the messenger that brought this dispatch," says the pamphlet, "who was an actor in that service, relates that the enemy marched away with such haste that they left their whole camp, which was very well furnished of all provisions of victual, store of wine, silks and velvet, scarlet and other cloth, both woollen and linen, and some money, all the cattle left in the quarters of Dublin as they found them there. Wednesday, the 8th, was appointed to be a day of thanksgiving in Dublin for this great victory." Besides the castles of Rathmines and Rathgar, Naas, Maynooth, and various other places, surrendered to Jones at that time. The Earl of Fingall and a brother of Ormond were among the prisoners, and it is said that Ormond himself narrowly escaped.

The news of this "great victory" reached Cromwell at Milford, and is noticed by him in letters written on ship-board when about to sail. About the middle of August, he "landed at Ringsend with 8,000 foot, 4,000 horse, a formidable train of artillery, and all other necessaries of war." In Dublin, he "was received with all possible demonstrations of joy; the great guns echoing forth their welcome, and the acclamations of the citizens resounding in every street. The Lord Lieutenant being come into the city—where the concourse of the citizens was very great, they all flocking to see him of whom they had heard so much—at a convenient place he made a stand, and with his hat in his hand, made a speech to them." This speech was entertained with great applause by the people, who all cried out, " We will live and die with you!"

Cromwell had nothing to detain him in Dublin, beyond making arrangements for governing the city, and for prosecuting the campaign on which he was about to enter: the rout of Ormond by Jones had cleared the way for him in the neighborhood of the metropolis. In a few days, he with his army marched towards Drogheda, where he promptly gave unmistakable and terrific proof of the course he had resolved to pursue. Carlyle describes it truly: " Oliver descended on Ireland like the hammer of Thor—smote it, as at one fell stroke, into dust and ruin, never to reünite against him more." " To him," Merle d'Aubigné says, " the most energetic way appeared the most humane." Even Sir Jonas Barrington writes of him, " Never was any rebel so triumphant as he was in Ireland; yet it is impossible to deny, that perhaps a less decisive or less cruel general than that splendid usurper, might by lenity have increased the misery in prolonging the warfare, and have lengthened out the sanguinary scenes of an unavailing resistance."

Owen did not accompany Cromwell to the country. He remained preaching in Dublin till, in a few months, through abundant labors in that and other ways, his health declined, and he returned to his pastorate at Coggeshall in Essex. In a sermon on "The Steadfastness of the Promises and the Sinfulness of Staggering," preached before the parliament, February 28th, 1649, he lays open the case of Ireland, and pleads in its behalf in a style worthy of himself. "How is it," he asks, "that Jesus Christ is in Ireland only as a lion staining all his garments with the blood of his enemies; and none to hold him out as a Lamb sprinkled with his own blood to his friends? Is it the sovereignty and interest of England that is alone to be there transacted? For my part, I see no further into the mystery of these things, but that I could heartily rejoice that, innocent blood being expiated, the Irish might enjoy Ireland so long as the moon endureth, so that Jesus Christ might possess the Irish." In urging his auditors to "do their utmost for the preaching of the gospel in Ireland," he pleads in this strain: "They want it. No want like theirs who want the gospel. I would there were for the present one gospel preacher for every walled town in the English possession in Ireland. The land mourneth, and the people perish for lack of knowledge: many run to and fro, but it is upon other designs: knowledge is not increased. They are sensible of their wants, and cry out for a supply. The tears and cries of the inhabitants of Dublin, after the manifestation of Christ, are ever in my view. If they were in the dark, and loved to have it so, it might something close a door upon the bowels of our compassion; but they cry out of their darkness, and are ready to follow every one whosoever to have a candle. If their being gospelless move not our hearts, it is hoped their importunate cries will disquiet our rest, and wrest help as a beggar doth alms," etc.

These appeals from Owen to the parliament told better for Ireland than did Lord Bacon's advice to Queen Elizabeth's secretary, half a century before. In the month after they were uttered, a bill was passed for vesting certain estates in the hands of trustees for the better support of Trinity College, the erection of a second college, the support of professors in the university, and the maintenance of a free-school; and on the same day the House resolved to "send over forthwith six able ministers to dispense the gospel in the city of Dublin."

Perhaps it is to the college and free-school whose erection was provided for by the above bill, or to that college and the one previously existing in Back lane, which had been taken from the Roman Catholics and connected with the university, that Fuller refers when he writes, "The whole species of the university of Dublin was for many years preserved in the *individuum* of this one college [Trinity]. But, since, this instrument hath made better music, when what was but a monochord before hath got two other smaller strings unto it—the addition of New College and Kildare Hall." Among the ministers sent over pursuant to the parliament's resolve was John Rogers, a man of much learning, exuberant fancy, and ardent piety, all apparent in his singular quarto entitled "A Tabernacle for the Sun."

Commissioners came from the parliament to

administer the affairs of Ireland, in 1651, and resided in Cork House. They were accompanied by the Reverend Samuel Winter, previously minister of Cottingham, in Yorkshire, whom they made provost of the College, which office he held till the Restoration. Calamy states that Winter relinquished a living of £400 a year in England, for a salary of £100, that he might promote the gospel in Ireland; also that Trinity College, which he found almost desolate, became under his care a valuable seminary of piety and learning. He was most indefatigable: besides presiding over the college, he was pastor of a church in the city, afternoon preacher at Christ Church, the principal service, had a sermon every Sunday morning in St. Nicholas's at seven o'clock, and preached ocsionally at Maynooth.

Many other ministers settled in Dublin during the Commonwealth, of whom the best known are Dr. Harrison, Stephen Charnock, author of the treatise on the "Divine Attributes," Samuel Mather, to whom we are indebted for a work on the "Types," being a collection of discourses delivered in Dublin after the Restoration, and John Murcot, a young man of great promise, and whose ministry seems to have been attended with signal power for usefulness in the city and other parts. From Murcot's Life, called "Moses in the Mount," in a posthumous volume of his works, we learn that people of the highest rank, as well as the public generally, flocked to hear him, and that both in the pulpit and in private he proved himself to be most earnest for the honor of God and the good of souls. Dr. Winter, with whom he was colleague in the ministry, in an Epistle Dedicatory to the Lord Deputy Fleetwood and the Lord Henry Cromwell, prefixed to the above volume, says of him, "his praise is in the gospel throughout all the churches: I have seldom known of his years a head better hearted, or a heart better headed; the enlargement of whose heart was the enlargement of his abilities." He died in December, 1654, not having completed his thirtieth year, and was buried in St. Mary's chapel, Christ Church: his funeral was attended by the lord deputy, his commissioners, the mayor, aldermen, and great numbers of the citizens.

Most persons are aware how nobly Oliver Cromwell espoused the cause of the persecuted Protestants in Piedmont. In July, 1655, a collection towards their relief was begun in Dublin, and in January the sum of £1,097 6s. 3d. was remitted for the purpose by parties belonging to Dr. Winter's church.

About the time we are now speaking of, associations by mutual agreement for common purposes were being formed in several parts of England, among the ministers of different denominations. The celebrated Richard Baxter was zealous in promoting them. Archbishop Usher approved of them. In their meetings one of the ministers presided as "moderator." Baxter, in his Life, writes that "the Independent churches also in Ireland, led on by Dr. Winter, pastor of their church in Dublin, associated with the moderate Presbyterians there, upon these provocations, and the persuasions of Colonel John Bridges." He gives a letter signed by Winter and other ministers, "In the name of the associated churches of Christ in Ireland. These for the Reverend Mr. Richard Baxter, pastor of the church of Christ in Kidderminster, to be by him communicated to the several churches of that association." The letter is dated July 5th, 1655, and breathes genuine Christian catholicity: "The present condition of God's people in foreign parts, as among us," say the writers, "calls aloud for a more cordial union and communion among all such who desire to fear His name. It is therefore our hearts' desire, not to be wanting in our faith and prayers, resolves and endeavors, to the fulfilling of those exceeding great and precious truths which do eminently centre in these latter days, *that Christ's friends may receive one mind and heart, to serve him with one lip and shoulder.* We are thereby much encouraged to request your Christian assistance and brotherly correspondency, that we may all be the better able, in our several stations and relations, to promote more vigorously the interest of Christ and his people. After the sad shakings of this land, and his many turnings of things upside down, the Lord is pleased to promise us a little reviving, and to open a door of hope, even in the valley of Achor. Your favorable help is therefore earnestly craved, that *Ireland* may once more partake of the glad tidings of heaven, and the wants of many thousand starving souls may be seasonably supplied with the bread of life." To the letter from which these sentences are taken, Baxter and four other ministers sent a long and cordial response, "In the name of the Associated Ministers meeting at Kidderminster, August 12th, 1655," inscribed, "to the Reverend our much-honored Brother Dr. Winter, Pastor of the Church of Dublin, to be communicated by him to the associated churches in Ireland: These." Under date of "Dublin, January 16th, 1655–6," a letter was sent to Baxter and his brethren, signed by Dr. Winter and five "Elders of the Church of Christ in Dublin, whereof Dr. Samuel Winter is Pastor," "In the name and by the appointment of the rest of the associated churches in Ireland."

Henry Cromwell was lord deputy at the time this correspondence was going on. He was a truly Christian man, and did much to promote the gospel in the country, and union between the followers of his and their Lord. At his invitation, a meeting of the principal ministers of different denominations, and from the several provinces of the country, was held in Dublin in April, 1648. About thirty were present, including three Presbyterians from the north of Ireland. "He requested their advice respecting the instruction and conversion of the Roman Catholic population, the promoting of peace and unity among all godly ministers though of different churches, the due observance of the Sabbath, and the suppression of heresy and profaneness." They remained for five weeks together, gave Henry their opinions on the topics he had proposed, presented to him an address, and then "returned to their respective homes, with much love, having, during the time of their being together, kept a good understanding and mutual respect and kindness towards one another."

The information we have of secular matters in Dublin, from Cromwell's arrival to the Restoration, is extremely meagre. Colonel Hewson was, in the early part of the time, governor of the city, and General Fleetwood lord deputy. In 1652, a court of justice was erected for the trial of persons concerned in the "barbarous murders" committed in the rebellion, and Sir Phelim O'Neil and others were condemned and executed. The city was tranquil and prosperous. Provision was made for victualling the government vessels as they lay near the city, the absence of which convenience had obliged them before to go elsewhere for supplies. A weekly postal communication was established with England, by packet to Holyhead.

Oliver Cromwell died early in September, 1658: his eldest son, Richard, succeeded him as protector, and was proclaimed in Dublin on the 10th. Henry was appointed lord lieutenant of Ireland by his brother Richard. "The kingdom continued to enjoy unusual tranquillity, and in no part of the empire did there exist a more cordial or general submission to the new protector." But Richard was unequal to his high and difficult position. He summoned a parliament in January, 1658-9, which he dissolved in April. The army induced him to resign. The remains of Oliver's last parliament assembled: the government of

Ireland was vested in commissioners, but Henry, anticipating his recall by the parliament, sent his resignation to the speaker, and retired from public life. Rapin gives it as the general opinion, that had Henry been made protector instead of Richard, the course of events afterwards would have been widely different from what it was. Early in May, four commissioners came from the parliament to Dublin, and continued undisturbed in power till January, 1659–60, when a party of general officers seized the castle, declared for a free parliament, and, upon petition from the mayor and aldermen of the city, summoned a convention which met in February.

While matters were going on thus in Dublin, measures were being taken in England which ended in an agreement that Charles II. should take the throne of Britain. He had, years before, sworn to the solemn league and covenant, and been crowned at Scone: he now promised all manner of good things as he thought might be agreeable to the parties who went to negotiate with him at Breda. On 14th May, 1660, his declaration was accepted by the convention in Dublin, and the authorities there concurred in his restoration. Soon afterwards, Sir Hardress Waller with his troops seized the castle for the parliament, but was obliged to surrender it after a siege of five days. By the close of the year, the "Restoration" was accomplished; lords justices were sworn in to administer the king's government in Ireland; and the Duke of Ormond came over as lord lieutenant the following year.

The ecclesiastical arrangements of Ireland now reverted to the position in which they were before the English parliament acquired the sovereignty of the country. Bramhall was appointed to the primacy, and six new bishops were consecrated for vacant sees. Nonconformists were ejected from the churches and the college, without waiting, as in England, for a new Act of Uniformity.

The college was a gainer by the Restoration. Archbishop Usher had died in 1655: his library, containing ten thousand volumes, which had cost him many thousand pounds, was, together with his collection of manuscripts, then offered for sale. The King of Denmark and Cardinal Mazarin sought to purchase it; but the officers and men of the parliamentary army in Ireland, nobly resolving that so great a treasure should not leave the country, raised among themselves the money requisite to secure it, and then freely assigned it for the new college which had been projected in the city. It was placed in the castle for safe custody. When Charles came to the throne, he made a present of it to Trinity College, and over the compartments which it occupies in the library, his royal *munificence* is commemorated by the following inscription: *"Bibliotheca Usseriana Ex Dono Serenissimi Regis Caroli Secundi."* Dr. Parr states that this contribution then made up the greater part of the college library.

During the year 1662, some of the nonconformist ministers who had formally resided in the city returned and regathered their congregations.

Of these were Samuel Mather and Dr. Harrison. The church of the former met in New Row, the other in Cooke street. A third congregation was formed in Wood street.

Among the occurrences of the city about this period, mentioned in its annals, are the gift of a collar of SS. to its chief magistrate by the king, in 1660, together with a foot company to protect his person and sustain his dignity. This was followed in 1665 by the title of "Lord Mayor," and £500 a year in lieu of the foot company. In October, 1666, the lord lieutenant and the council "considered about sending 105,000 bullocks for the relief of London, lately burnt;" but whether they did the generous deed is not explained. The next year, through an apprehension of invasion from France, the militia were enrolled; and that year was further remarkable for the birth of the celebrated Dean Swift, in Hoey's court, near the castle, the houses in which were then handsome residences, though now in extreme dilapidation. In 1670, "in consequence of a great storm at new moon, the river overflowed up to Lazar's Hill, now Brunswick street, and the college." St. Stephen's Green was enclosed and drained, and a double row of lime trees planted along the wall. New pipes were laid for supplying the city with water. Bells were hung in St. Patrick's, Christ Church, and St. Catharine's. Essex bridge was erected in 1676.

Not long subsequent to the Restoration, the leaders of the Roman Catholics were on the alert to engage the king to fulfil the stipulations made to them in the peace concluded between his father and the confederates, in 1648-9. A toleration was in consequence granted them, but not to the extent desired. Shortly after this, the plot of Titus Oates, in England, created alarm in Ireland. Stringent courses were taken by the authorities against the "papists." All Roman Catholic ecclesiastics were ordered to quit the country, and no person of their persuasion was allowed to enter the castle. The titular archbishop of Dublin was thrown into prison. Proclamation was made to seize and confine the relations of "Tories," till the principals were killed or apprehended; also to incarcerate the parish priest on occasions when a robbery had been committed.

Charles II. died on February 6th, 1684: James II. was proclaimed in Dublin on the 11th. In the same year, "the Royal Hospital of Kilmainham, at the west end of Dublin, was built at the charge of the army, being a very spacious, stately, and commodious building, for aged and maimed soldiers, who are here well maintained," says Harris, "to the number of about four hundred." Ormond and Arran bridges were also erected.

In January, 1685, the Earl of Clarendon succeeded the Duke of Ormond as lord lieutenant, and having held office twelve months, was superseded by the Earl of Tyrconnel. This nobleman had already, while having command of the troops as lieutenant general, made the army, as far as possible, Roman Catholic; and now proceeded more thoroughly to fulfil his royal master's will, and to promote the interests of his Church, in the exercise of his new powers. But he had one aim which he did not dare to avow. He secretly negotiated for separating Ireland from the British crown, and placing it under the protectorate of France. Protestants were removed from the highest law offices, and Roman Catholics appointed in their room. The municipal corporations were cajoled, on various pretexts and promises, to give up their charters, in order to new ones being granted, and if they objected, were pursued with a *quo warranto*. By this means, the local civil authorities throughout the country became Roman Catholic. Large provisions were made for the Roman Catholic prelates; and dispensations were granted to Protestant Episcopal ministers who embraced Romanism, to retain their benefices, notwithstanding their apostasy, of which a signal instance occurred in Peter Manby, the dean of Derry. In April, 1687, came out James's "Declaration of Liberty of Conscience," by his sole prerogative suspending the execution of the penal laws against Roman Catholics and Dissenters. It extended to Ireland, and was met by addresses of approval, thanks, and professions of loyalty from almost all parties in the country; among others, under the head of "Windsor, June 20," the London Gazette mentions that "An Address from the Presbyterian ministers and the congregations in and near the city of Dublin, was transmitted hither by his excellency the Earl of Tyrconnel, lord deputy of Ireland; with another address presented to his excellency on the same subject by those of the Congregational persuasion, in behalf of themselves and others meeting in New Row, in Dublin; both which were very graciously received by his majesty." And in a July Gazette is recorded an address from his majesty's "Dissenting subjects in Munster," and another from the "Presbyterian ministers of Ulster." In fact, that official organ, number after number, so teemed with announcements of these effusions, that one might suppose there was hardly a difference of opinion in the country on the subject to which they referred.

Now came the memorable year 1688. The reader is referred to histories of England for details of the measures which ended in the substitution of William, Prince of Orange, for his father-in-law, James II., on the throne of these realms—an issue that secured much of what had been struggled for, but not permanently obtained, thirty years before. It is said that Tyrconnel had private knowledge of proceedings with William before James was acquainted with them, and that James received his earliest intimation of them from his Irish lord deputy. James at first treated the movement with contempt, but he soon was made to feel that it was a substantive and strong reality, before which he and his principles had to quail.

William arrived at Torbay on the 4th of November, and, before the end of December, James left the kingdom and retired to France. A convention of the lords and commons of England adjudged that he had, *ipso facto*, abdicated the throne, which they then offered to William, Prince of Orange, and his princess Mary, James's daughter. The offer was accepted. Ireland had no share in that transaction: Tyrconnel held that country for James. While the English convention were presenting the crown to William and Mary, Tyrconnel was disarming all the Protestants of Dublin and other places over which his power extended. The churches of the city were made dépôts: Trinity College was converted into a barrack. Sir Thomas Hacket, the lord mayor, Colonel Lutrel, the governor of Dublin, and the lord chief justice Nugent, emulated the lord lieutenant in zeal against the Protestants. On the 12th of March, King James landed at Kinsale, reached Dublin on the 24th, and called a parliament, which sat till July 20th. Among other doings, it repealed the Act of Settlement, and passed an Act of Attainder against two thousand six hundred Protestants. King, dean of St. Patrick's and *locum tenens* of the archbishop, then absent, was repeatedly imprisoned, and in great danger through his steadfastness, when the Protestants were proscribed.

To provide for his necessities James established a mint in Dublin, for coining money out of the worst kind of brass, old guns, and other refuse metal, melted down together. The mass was worth from threepence to fourpence a pound-weight; and by proclamation, dated June 18th, this money was made current, twenty shillings of it not being worth more than twopence. Of this base coin nearly 390,000 *pounds weight* were struck and made to pass for the value of nearly

1,600,000 *pounds sterling*, in what were called half-crowns, shillings, and sixpences. In this money the troops were paid, and all business transacted. A coinage of pewter was prepared the next year, but the final defeat of James prevented its being issued.

On the 3d May, 1690, Lutrel, governor of Dublin, issued an order commanding all ministers and curates of the several parishes in the city and liberties to send in the names of all male Protestants and Dissenters in the several parishes, by the following Thursday, under pain of being treated as spies or enemies. On the 18th, he issued another, requiring all Protestants who were not housekeepers, or who had not followed some lawful vocation for three months before, to depart within twenty-four hours, under pain of death or imprisonment; and all Protestants not of the privy council, nor in the king's army or actual service, to deliver up within the said time their arms and ammunition into the stores, on pain of death. He further ordered that no Protestant presume to walk the streets from ten o'clock at night till five in the morning, nor at any time during an alarm; and that no greater number of them than five should meet and converse at any time, either in houses, streets, or fields, under pain of death, or such punishment as a court-martial should think fit. He also made disobedience to many of his verbal orders death. But deliverance was at hand.

On the day before the last-named edict was issued, King William landed at Carrickfergus, near

Belfast. Some of his officers suggested the propriety of remaining for some time in that neighborhood, but he said, with a degree of warm resolve, "I came not to Ireland to let the grass grow under my feet." He at once marched southward. On Tuesday, July 1, he routed James's army in the battle of the Boyne, and the next day took possession of Drogheda. James hastened to Dublin after the battle, called together the council and magistrates, and gave them a farewell address, representing that his Irish troops were not to be depended on, that fortune was against him, and that he should now shift for himself, as they also must do. He charged them not to burn or pillage the city, and concluded by promising to labor for their deliverance as long as he lived. The next morning he left, accompanied by the Dukes of Berwick and Tyrconnel and the Marquis of Powis, for Waterford, whence he embarked for France. On his departure, the principal Roman Catholics fled from Dublin; the Protestants possessed themselves of the militia arms, formed a committee of management, despatched letters to King William with an account of what had transpired, and invited his presence in the metropolis. On Saturday the 5th, William encamped at Finglass, and the next day, Sunday, he "rode," says Rapin, "in a triumphant manner into Dublin, and went directly to St. Patrick's Church, the cathedral of that metropolis, attended by the bishops of Meath and Limerick; and after the public services were solemnly performed, Dr. King, afterwards archbishop of Dublin, preached a sermon upon the power and wisdom of the providence of God, in protecting his people, and defeating their enemies. The mayor and aldermen waited on his majesty; and the people endeavored, by all demonstrations of joy, to express their just sense of their great and happy deliverance. In the afternoon, the king returned to the camp." On the Monday, he published a royal declaration, promising pardon and protection to all who returned and submitted, excepting the leaders in the outrages that had been perpetrated, and even holding out hope to them by an assurance that he would never refuse mercy to those who were truly penitent. On Wednesday, July 9th, the king removed the greater part of his army to Crumlin, two miles south of the city, and despatched the remainder of his forces towards Athlone. On the next day, he issued a proclamation, annulling that of James respecting the base money, and reducing its current value to its real worth. Having appointed brigadier Trelawny to the command in Dublin, William advanced as far as Inchiquin, twenty-two miles on his way to Kilkenny. Towards the end of the month, he came back from Carrick-on-Suir to Dublin, and stayed at Chapel-Izod some days, hearing complaints and redressing grievances. He rejoined the army on the 4th of August, and, having besieged Limerick, he appointed lords justices, and sailed for England from Duncannon Fort, about the 1st of September.

The next year's campaign brought the war in

Ireland to a close. The city of Dublin, "in grateful commemoration of their late deliverance by the conduct and valor of King William III., erected his statue on horseback," in College Green, bearing a Latin inscription. It was inaugurated with great solemnity, on July the 1st, 1701, being the anniversary of the victory of the Boyne.

Until the past few years, this statue was wont to be newly gilt and painted for the same anniversary. Its new adorning, however, provoked assault and defence between partisans, contests which frequently ended in bloodshed. Its annual decoration, therefore, has given place to an enduring coat of bronze, and it is allowed to stand longer than the twelvemonth round in quietness, unharmed itself, and without offence being given or taken from it among any of the passers by.

SECTION VI.

DUBLIN IN THE EIGHTEENTH CENTURY.

A LONDON bookseller, who had crossed the Atlantic, and was generally acquainted with men and things, spent some time in Dublin about the commencement of the eighteenth century. His name was John Dunton. He has given a pretty full account of Trinity College, as then circumstanced.

"It consists," he writes, "of three squares, the outward being as large as both the inner, one of which, of modern building, has not chambers on every side—the other has; on the south side of which stands the library, the whole length of the square. The hall and butteries run the same range with the library, and separates the two inner squares. It is an old building; as is also the Regent House, which from a gallery looks into the chapel, which has been of late years enlarged, being before too little for the number of scholars, who are now, with the fellows, etc., reckoned about three hundred and forty. They have a garden for the fellows, and another for the provost, both neatly kept; as also a bowling-green, and large parks for the students to walk and exercise in. The foundation consists of a provost; seven senior fellows, of whom two are doctors in divinity; eight juniors, to whom one is lately added; and seventy scholars." A new house was then building for the provost, which was to be "very noble and magnificent." The same writer speaks of being shown " the gardens belonging to the college, which were very pleasant and entertaining. Here was a sun-dial, on which might be seen what o'clock it was in most parts of the world. This dial was placed upon the top of a stone, representing a pile of books. And not far from this was another sun-dial, set in a box, of a very large compass, the gnomon of it being very near as big as a barber's pole. Leaving this pleasant garden, we ascended several steps, which brought us into a curious walk, where we had a prospect to the west of the city, and to the east of the sea and harbor: on the south we could see the mountains of Wicklow, and on the north, the river Liffey, which runs by the side of the college." He says, " the library is over the scholars' lodgings, the length of one of the quadrangles, and contains a great many choice books of great value, particularly one, the largest I ever saw for breadth: it was a 'Herbal,' containing the lively portraitures of all sorts of trees, plants, herbs, and flowers." There also he saw what seem to have been the germs of a museum: among other curiosities, "the thigh-bone of a giant," "kept there as a convincing demonstration of the vast bigness which some human bodies have in former times arrived to." "At the east end of this library, on the right hand, is a chamber called the 'Countess of Bath's Library,' filled with many handsome folios and other books, in Dutch binding, gilt, with the earl's arms impressed upon them; for he had been some time in this house. On the left hand, opposite to this room, is another chamber, in which I saw a great many manuscripts, medals, and other curiosities. At the west end of the library, there is a division made by a kind of wooden lattice-work, containing about thirty paces, full of choice and curious books, which was the library of that great man, Archbishop Usher." "The library, at present, is but an ordinary pile of building, and cannot be distinguished on the outside; but I hear they design the building of a new library; and I am told the House of Commons in Ireland have voted three thousand pounds towards carrying it on."

Dunton mentions it as customary to read publicly in the chapel of the college, every Trinity Sunday, in the afternoon, the name of Queen Elizabeth, and of every other contributor to it from its foundation, "as a grateful acknowledgment to the memory of their benefactors." He then describes the proceedings which took place on the first hundredth anniversary of its opening, a few years before his visit. "On the 9th of January, 1693, (which completed a century from the foundation of the college,) they celebrated their first secular day, when the provost, Dr. Ashe, now Bishop of Clogher, preached, and made a notable entertainment for the lords justices, lord mayor, and aldermen of Dublin. The sermon preached by the provost was on the subject of the foundation of the college; and his text was, Matt. xxvi. 13, 'Verily I say unto you, Wheresoever this gospel shall be preached in the whole world, there shall also this, that this woman hath done, be told for a memorial of her:' which in this sermon the provost applied to Queen Elizabeth, the foundress of the college. The sermon was learned and ingenious, and afterwards printed by Mr. Ray, and dedicated to the lords justices. In the afternoon, there were several orations in Latin, spoke by the scholars, in praise of Queen Elizabeth and the succeeding princes; and an ode made by Mr. Tate, (the Poet Laureate,) who was bred up in this college. Part of the ode was this following:—

> Great parent, hail! all hail to thee;
>   Who hast the last distress survived,
>   To see this joyful day arrived,
> The Muses' second jubilee.
>
> Another century commencing,
>   No decay in thee can trace:
> Time, with his own law dispensing,
>   Adds new charms to every grace
>   That adorns thy youthful face.
>
> After war's alarms repeated,
> And a circling age completed,
>   Numerous offspring thou dost raise,
>   Such as to Juverna's praise
> Shall Liffey make as proud a name
> As that of Isis or of Cam.

Awful matron, take thy seat
  To celebrate this festival:
The learn'd assembly well to treat,
  Bless'd Eliza's days recall:
    The wonders of her reign recount,
    In strains that Phœbus may surmount,
Songs for Phœbus to repeat.
    She 'twas that did at first inspire,
    And tune the mute Hibernian lyre.

Succeeding princes next recite:
With never-dying verse requite
  Those favors they did shower.
'Tis this alone can do them right:
To save them from oblivion's night,
  Is only in the Muse's power.

But chiefly recommend to Fame,
Maria and great William's name,
  Whose isle to him her freedom owes;
And surely no Hibernian Muse
Can her restorer's praise refuse,
  While Boyne or Shannon flows.

"After this ode had been sung by the principal gentlemen of the kingdom, there was a very diverting speech made in English by the *Terræ Filius*. The night concluded with illuminations, not only in the college, but in other places."

Thus was celebrated the "first secular day," or hundredth anniversary, of the Dublin University. The same informant, speaking of the viceregal court, says of the lords justices, "When they go to church, the streets, from the castle gate to the church door, as also the great aisle of the church, to the foot of the stairs by which they ascend to the place where they sit, are lined with soldiers.

They are preceded by the pursuivants of the council-chamber, two maces, and, on state-days, by the king and pursuivant-at-arms, their chaplains, and gentlemen of the household, with pages and footmen bareheaded. When they alight from their coach, in which commonly the lord chancellor and one of the prime nobility sit with them, the sword of state is delivered to some lord to carry before them. And in the like manner they return back to the castle, where the several courses at dinner are ushered in by kettle-drums and trumpets."

Upon the revocation of the Edict of Nantes, many French Protestants came over to Ireland. Their numbers were increased by the officers and men of a Huguenot regiment which served under William III., and, on being disbanded, remained in the country. Their principal location was Portarlington, in the Queen's county, where they formed so large and influential a proportion of the inhabitants, that French became the common language of the place. Not a few of them, however, settled in the metropolis, and proved an important accession to its general intelligence, refinement, industry, and moral worth. The names of French street, Digges street, Aungier street, etc., tell their origin, and those of La Touche and other respectable families indicate their descent. These refugees, in 1695, formed three congregations: two of them Calvinistic, who worshipped in Peter street and Lucas lane, and the other, consisting of persons who preferred a liturgical service, had the use of a chapel in St. Patrick's Cathedral. A

German regiment had also been engaged in Ireland under William. On the war of the revolution being ended, this corps went to the continent, but when it was disbanded at the peace of Ryswick, portions belonging to it came over to Dublin with their chaplain, and formed a German Lutheran congregation, which had a place of worship in Marlborough street. The government of that period greatly encouraged the settlement of foreign Protestants in Ireland. The Nonconformists also had obtained comparative security and freedom. Under the general name of "Protestant Dissenters," they had in Dublin seven congregations, four Presbyterian, two Independent or Congregational, and one Baptist.

Dr. Narcissus Marsh had been Archbishop of Dublin from 1694 to 1702, in which year he was translated to Armagh. He died in 1713. "While he governed the Church in Dublin," writes Harris, "he built a noble library, near the palace of St. Sepulchre's, which he enlarged after his translation to Armagh, and filled it with a choice collection of books, having for that purpose bought the library of Doctor Edward Stillingfleet, formerly Bishop of Worcester, to which he added his own collection. And to make it more useful to the public, he plentifully endowed a librarian and sub-librarian to attend to it at certain prescribed hours. It is estimated that, besides the endowment, which amounted to two hundred and fifty pounds a year, he expended more than four thousand pounds in the building and books; and to make every thing secure to perpetuity, he obtained an act of parliament for the settling and preserving it." Harris adds, "I am under the necessity of acknowledging, from a long experience, that this is the only useful library in the kingdom, being open to all strangers, and at all reasonable times." This library is chiefly valuable for works published prior to its founder's death, only ten pounds annually being available for providing additions except what are obtained by donation. Harris wrote in 1739. Marsh's library, though a most munificent boon to the city, has long ceased to be "the only useful library in the kingdom." It is not at present resorted to as it once was, partly from its locality and from its worth not being known, but principally from other libraries in the city, including those of the University and the Dublin Royal Society, being made nearly as accessible.

The reign of William III., many as were its advantages to the empire, was not, in all its measures, an unmixed good to Ireland. The fault, however, lay with a portion of his subjects, rather than with the king himself, who seems to have acted, in the case we are about to allude to, more from compulsion than from choice. In Henry the Third's time, and afterwards, the woollen manufactures of Ireland were much sought after in England, and were admitted there duty free. Their excellence was such that the Irish serges won for themselves the epithet of "noble" in Italy; and in 1482, the pope's agent at the English court asked and obtained, from Richard II., permission to export woollen mantles from Ireland for his own dominions on the same terms. The trade went on more or less prospering, though of course affected by circumstances, till the latter half of the seventeenth century, when it began to excite jealousy among parties engaged in the same manufacture in England. The restoration of quietness and confidence in Ireland after the revolution, induced a number of English capitalists to come and establish themselves in that line in Dublin, where labor was cheap, and other conditions existed advantageous for carrying it on. Several streets in the "Liberty," and with them the "Weaver's square," were then built, and soon became the residence of much opulence and respectability. The success of this enterprise greatly increased the umbrage, and even produced alarm, in interested parties on the other side of the channel. The latter betook themselves to their parliament. Both the lords and the commons of England petitioned the king to interfere, and check the progress of the woollen trade in Ireland. He accordingly wrote to the lords justices, and by governmental influence induced the Irish parliament to impose a duty of twenty per cent. on broadcloth exported from Ireland, and of half that amount on serges and baize. This sudden suppression of the Irish woollen manufacture was disastrous to Dublin in the highest degree. Multitudes were reduced to beggary, both in the metropolis and the country. Happily the incubus then placed on Irish industry has long since been removed, and the energy and skill of both countries may now, so far as government is concerned, be put forth at will in friendly competition on equal terms, in any of the world's markets.

The Irish parliament having thus nearly destroyed the woollen manufacture of their country, sought to make amends for the mischief by encouraging that of linen. The ancient Irish were so partial to their linen as an article for clothing, that, under Henry VIII., laws were enacted limiting the quantity to seven yards for a garment, in making which thirty had previously been employed: the reason of this interference does not appear; but, as we have already seen, the Irish parliament at a later period regarded the "dress" of the people as within the province of legislative cognizance. Whatever censure may justly attach to Wentworth, Earl of Strafford, it is not to be denied that he was a great and lasting benefactor to Ireland in one particular. Observing, when lord deputy, of how much advantage to the country the linen manufacture might become, and how well adapted the soil was for the growth of flax, he devoted *thirty thousand* pounds of his own money to promote the culture of the plant and the increase of the trade. By an act of the eighth year of Queen Anne, a board of trustees was constituted with extensive powers for advancing the manufacture and sale of linens. They first rented a room on Cork Hill as their place of business; but that accommodation being soon too small, apartments were assigned them in the castle. By the year 1719 the erection of a "Linen Weaver's Hall in or near the city of Dublin," was resolved on, parliament voting £3000 towards the undertaking. On the 14th of November, 1728, the great linen hall at the top of Capel street was opened by public advertisement. For many years it presented all the stir of a first-rate mart; but, through changes in mercantile intercourse, it is now deserted and pervaded by the stillness of a sepulchre, so far as regards occupation for its original purpose.

French refugees brought the silk manufacture to London; and to their brethren who settled in Dublin, as already described, that city owes its "Spitalfields." The progress of this branch of trade will be noticed hereafter.

We have mentioned the birth of Swift. It was in 1713 that he became Dean of St. Patrick's. Neither his general conduct nor his writings were always consistent with his profession as a minister of religion, yet he is said to have made some reforms in the chapter of his cathedral, and he proved himself earnest for his country. In 1720, he acquired great popularity by publishing "A Proposal for the Universal Use of Irish Manufactures." That, however, was not the chief service he rendered to the public. In the year 1722, the Duchess of Kendal obtained through Lord Sunderland an exclusive patent for coining half-pence and farthings for Irish circulation, to the amount of £100,800, and then sold the patent to a person of the name of Wood, at Wolverhampton. Wood, to make the best of his bargain, prepared a coinage of the basest metal, striking off a few of the standard value, as specimens for approval at the Mint in London. The whole power of the government was engaged to force the new coinage on the Irish public. Archbishop King protested; but Swift wielded his pen, under the assumed name of M. B. Drapier, with resistless force against it, in four letters, during the year 1724. The authorities offered a reward of "three hundred pounds" (the largest that had ever been offered) for the discovery of the writer, but in vain. The printer was seized; but the grand jury ignored the bill, notwithstanding that the violence of a corrupt judge was exerted to induce them to send the case for trial. The next grand juries of Dublin city and county proscribed all such persons as should attempt to impose Wood's coin upon the kingdom, as enemies of his majesty's government, and acknowledged "with all just gratitude, the services of such patriots as had been eminently zealous in detecting this fraudulent imposition, and preventing the passing of this base coin." At length, the government, in September, 1725, found themselves unable to continue the struggle, and refrained from any further attempt towards making the people submit to the gross and scandalous imposition. The "Drapier" had been throughout known, though not betrayed. He now came forth from his retreat, beloved, revered, idolized, as the deliverer of his country. At his death, in 1744, he bequeathed a large portion of his property to found a hospital for lunatics and idiots. As he advanced in years, his own mind gave way, and he became a fit object for an asylum, such as he was providing for others. The hospital was begun in 1749, and finished in 1757.

Previous to the founding of Swift's Hospital, several other public buildings, besides the Linen Hall, had been completed, or at least commenced, in Dublin, since the century began. Of these may be named the Workhouse, (changed in 1730 into a foundling hospital,) and the Royal Barracks, in 1704; in which year also the Castle Market was opened by the civic authorities with "beat of drum." The foundation of a new Custom House, on what is now Wellington Quay, was laid in 1707. In 1720, Stevens's Hospital was begun; in 1728, the "Charitable Infirmary" on Inn's Quay, now the hospital in Jervis street, was founded; in 1729, the "North Wall," and in 1748, the South Wall from Ringsend, were commenced. In 1732, the building of the College Library, which was preparing for early in the century, as before noticed, was finished, as was also the Mercer's Hospital in the year following, on what had been the site of St. Stephen's Church. But the principal undertaking of this period was the erection of a building for the accommodation of the parliament. The foundation of this magnificent structure—which since its completion has stood almost unrivalled, for its size, in dignified simplicity and elegance—was laid in 1729. The site chosen for it was College Green. The main portion of the building was completed in ten years afterwards, at an expense of £40,000.* In 1785, an eastern front was added to afford a separate entrance for the lords, who, however, showed their authority more than their good taste in requiring that its columns should be adorned with Corinthian capitals, instead of Ionic as in the rest of the building. This exception in the architecture is the only blemish in the edifice. Two years afterwards, a western front was supplied, but the example of the lords was not followed, the capitals being Ionic. These additional fronts cost, the eastern £25,000, and the western £30,000.

A Royal College of Physicians had been established by charter from Charles II., renewed by William III.; but the metropolis of Ireland had no general institution for advancing science and the arts previously to 1731. In that year, several gentlemen, of whom the most active were Dr.

---

* John Wesley, in his Journal for August 21, 1747, thus speaks of Dublin: "The town has scarce any public building, except the Parliament House, which is at all remarkable. The churches are poor and mean, both within and without. St. Stephen's Green might be made a beautiful place, being abundantly larger than Lincoln's Inn Square; but the houses round about it (besides that some are low and bad) are quite irregular, and unlike each other; and little care is taken of the Green itself, which is as rough and uneven as a common. (It was so then.) The college contains two little quadrangles, and one about as large as that of New College, in Oxford. There is likewise a bowling-green, a small garden, and a little park, and a new-built, handsome library."—EDITOR.

Samuel Madden and Mr. Thomas Prior, formed a voluntary association, for which, in 1749, a charter was obtained from George II., under the name of the Royal Dublin Society. Its specific object was to promote husbandry and other useful arts in Ireland; but it affords to its members the advantages of a general literary as well as scientific establishment. It now occupies the once ducal palace of Leinster, in Kildare street, containing an excellent library; two museums, one general, the other agricultural; a reading-room, lecture-room, and board-room; with schools of design in painting, sculpture, and the fine arts. It has professors of chemistry, geology, botany, natural philosophy, etc. Its extensive and well-furnished Botanic Garden at Glasnevin is surpassed by few in the world.

A French tourist, giving an account of Ireland in 1734, says: "The better to judge of this people in matters of learning, I have passed some hours in a bookseller's shop, whereof there are a great many in the capital, (Dublin.) I found there is no city in Europe (*cæteris paribus*) where there are so many good pieces printed, and so few bad. They do not believe this; but it is because they do not know what is done in other places. Printing and books are cheaper here than in London, but dearer than in Holland, and near a par with France. English editions are sold at the same rate as in London. But the prices of foreign books are exorbitant, and pass all bounds, the prime cost whereof in Holland, whether they be bought new, or at auctions, is very moderate, and a mere trifle. Coffeehouses here are much frequented: they have the best English papers, the "Amsterdam Gazette," and three good newspapers, taken out of the English, of their own. After the four capitals of Europe, Paris, London, Rome, and Amsterdam, Dublin, I think, may take place. It is a very large, populous, and well-built city. It stands on near as much ground as Amsterdam, and would take an oval wall of six miles and a half to encompass it. According to the manuscript account (taken in 1733) of all the several baronies and counties in the kingdom of Ireland, as the same were returned, and are now remaining in his Majesty's Surveyor-General's office, there are twelve thousand houses in Dublin, which at the rate of ten persons to a house, makes the number of inhabitants amount to one hundred and twenty thousand. The river Liffey, over which there are five stone bridges, runs through the middle of the city: ships of good burthen come up to the lowermost bridge, and unload at the Custom House quay. From this bridge there is a noble view down the river, which is always full of vessels; and in winter evenings, when all the lamps are lighted, you have three long vistas, resembling fireworks, both up and down the river, and before your face as you pass the bridge from the old town. The outlets of Dublin into fine fields, the banks of the river, a royal park, the seashore, etc., are very beautiful; and in this far exceed London, and indeed most other cities in Europe which I have seen."

The "three good newspapers" referred to above,

as then published in Dublin, were "Pue's Occurrences," begun in 1700, the first Irish newspaper; the "Dublin Gazette," and "Faulkner's Dublin Journal. Essex bridge was then the lowest on the river. The "long vista" before you as you passed over this bridge from the "old town" is Capel street. What would this tourist have said had he come again a century later, and stood on Carlisle bridge, with Sackville street, containing the Post-Office, Nelson's Pillar, and the Rotunda, northwards—the lines of quays, with bridge after bridge succeeding, up the river towards the Four Courts and the Park, westwards—other lines of quays down the river, with the splendid Custom-House, and crowds of vessels, including steamers not a few, and the North Wall Lighthouse, eastwards—Westmoreland street, terminating with the Bank, the University, and College Green, southwards—and d'Olier street branching off to the south-east—and all these ranges well lighted through their whole extent every evening, not with the dingy oil-tins of that now olden time, but with the brilliant gas which modern science and art have given?

Handel is yet held in remembrance, and will be till the loftiest strains of human music give place to those yet loftier of the perfected redeemed myriads before the throne of God and the Lamb. Dublin is interestingly associated with Handel's history. Fishshamble street is now abandoned to the occupancy of trunk-sellers and such like crafts: a century ago, it was a resort of the fashionables of the city. There yet stands, within a courtyard, what was the Deanery-house of Christ Church Cathedral, now a parish school and workhouse; and lower down a building mean, neglected, and in decay, not long since a theatre, but before that a Music-hall, erected by the subscriptions of a charitable musical society, and opened on the 2d of October, 1741. Here a musical academy, whose members were amateurs, exclusively moving in the first classes of society, held its meetings, under the presidency of the Earl of Mornington, father of the Duke of Wellington, as leader of the band. To Lord Mornington we are indebted for the tune called "*Ferns,*" one of the most exquisite that taste has supplied to aid the utterance of devotion. About six weeks after the opening of the Music-hall, Handel came to Dublin on the invitation of the Lord Lieutenant, the Duke of Devonshire. By the "Account" lately published, it appears that he prepared his well-known production, "The Messiah," in prospect of his visit to the Irish metropolis, and that this incomparably grand composition, including the "Hallelujah Chorus," and "Worthy is the Lamb," in which earthly music seems to have reached the *ne plus ultra* of its wondrous power, was first performed in the Music Hall, Fishshamble street, on Tuesday, the 13th of April, 1742, "for the relief of prisoners in the several jails, and for the support of the Mercer's Hospital,.and of the Charitable Infirmary on Inn's Quay." The proceeds on the occasion amounted to upwards of £400, or $2000.

The "Society of Friends" had formed congregations in Ireland during the Commonwealth, and were numerous at the time of the Revolution. Early in this century those in Dublin were subject to gross molestations; but after a while they obtained protection. In the year 1727, their yearly meeting in Dublin recorded on its minutes a "declaration of censure upon *the practice of importing negroes from their native country.*" The first record of a similar resolution in England was from the yearly meeting in London, in 1758. Hence it appears that the public movement against that traffic began in Dublin.

Subsequently to the revolution, and particularly on the threatened invasion by the Pretender in 1715, severe penal statutes were enforced against Roman Catholics. Among them were some to prevent the celebration of their worship. Whatever was done in administering its ritual, had to be performed privately and by stealth. No chapels were permitted, and the priest moved his altar, books, and every thing necessary for the celebration of his religious rites, from house to house, among such of his flock as were enabled in this way to support an itinerant domestic chaplain; while for the poorer some wash-house or stable, in a remote and retired situation, was selected, and here the service was silently and secretly performed, unobserved by the public eye." In consequence, however, of serious accidents frequently occurring to parties thus crowded together, combined with a disposition to less severity on the part of the government, the Lord Lieutenant, Lord Chesterfield, in 1745, permitted the congregations to assemble in more safe and public places. Chapels which had been long closed were reopened, and several new ones were subsequently built.

But Ireland has given many proofs that neither the persecution, nor the toleration, of a false religion by the civil authorities, insures the predominance of true piety in the community. Among the Protestant denominations, established or otherwise, in Dublin and in the country, at the period we write of, formalism was the order of the day. Early in the century, when Emlyn, co-pastor with Boyse in Wood street, avowed his disbelief in the deity of Christ, Boyse and the other Dissenting ministers, Presbyterian and Independent, proved their firm and zealous faith in that great truth. Afterwards John Leland, who had been ordained co-pastor with Nathaniel Weld, in the New Row congregation, since removed to Eustace street, was honorably distinguishing himself by his various writings in defence of Christianity against the determined assaults made upon it by the leading skeptics of the age. But by the middle of the century, when Leland was thus earnestly caring for the outworks of the gospel, complete listlessness towards the doctrines which are its life and strength and glory as a revelation of salvation by grace through faith to depraved and guilty and perishing men, was settling like a death-chill upon the dissenters of the metropolis, and upon the generality of their brethren elsewhere. And from the account given by the editor of the Life and Times of the Countess of Huntingdon, of the parochial or conforming clergy of that period, it appears that vital godliness was well-nigh quite extinct.

Such was the deplorable state of things affecting the highest and everlasting state of its inhabitants, when it pleased God, who commanded the light to shine out of darkness, to bring among them some of his servants bearing the light of the knowledge of his glory in the face of Jesus Christ.

The first of these faithful men was George Whitefield. His sphere of ministry embraced the countries speaking the English language on both sides of the Atlantic. With an eloquence which now flashed and rolled like the elements in a thunder-storm, and then tenderly beamed forth like the sun-ray on the flowers whose head the storm had drenched and made to droop, did he enforce on the people the truths which, under the guidance of the Messrs. Wesley, he had gathered out of God's precious word. The holiness of God as a Being of purer eyes than to behold iniquity: the perfect excellence of the divine law; its demand of entire obedience; its adaptation, if observed, to promote the happiness of man; its spirituality, reaching to the most secret thoughts and affections of the heart: the corruption of human nature: the alienation of man from God, and his moral inability to keep the divine law: the sentence of everlasting condemnation, which, as the awful but righteous consequence, falls upon our race: the marvellous kindness of God in so commending his love to us, "that while we were yet sinners Christ died for us:" the perfect satisfaction for sin rendered by his atoning sacrifice: the unutterable condescension and infinite love with which he receiveth sinners: the grace of the Holy Spirit: the necessity of an entire regeneration of the soul by his divine agency: forgiveness through the blood of Christ offered to all who believe: the universal obligation of repentance: the requirement of holiness of heart and life, as the evidence of love to Christ, and the indwelling of the Spirit, as the author of holiness: such were the grand truths which were proclaimed by the Wesleys, Whitefield, and their coadjutors—derisively called Methodists—and which, in numerous instances, fell with startling power on ears unaccustomed to evangelical statements and appeals.

Whitefield's first visit to Ireland was what would be called accidental. On his return from America in 1738, the vessel put into the Shannon in distress. He went to Limerick, introduced himself as a clergyman, and preached in the cathedral. Thence he came to Dublin, where his name and fame had preceded him, and he was most kindly received by some leading dignitaries of the Church. He preached in St. Werburgh's and St. Andrew's, to large congregations, with an effect unknown in the city before. This visit was followed by others. When in Dublin in 1757, he preached in the open air on Oxmantown Green, and was in imminent danger through the violence of the mob, who stoned and otherwise illtreated him. On this he remarked, that "when he first came to Dublin the people received him as a gentleman, but at his last appearance among them they treated him as an apostle."

Early in 1747, a minister connected with Mr. Wesley's part of the great movement, arrived and preached statedly in the chapel in Marlborough street, originally built for the use of the German Lutherans. Afterwards, Mr. Wesley himself came; and notwithstanding much opposition, his followers increased till, in 1756, they built the chapel until lately occupied by them in Whitefriars street. Mr. Wesley often visited Ireland: after a conference in Dublin in 1790, he left it never to return.*

A church of the United Brethren was formed in 1750, by the Rev. Messrs. Cennick and Latrobe, who erected the premises still held by that body in Bishop street.

At a somewhat later date, the Rev. Walter Shirley, rector of Loughrea, and the Rev. Richard De Courcy, afterwards vicar of St. Alkmond's, Shrewsbury, visited the city, and occasionally, but with great difficulty, had access to the parochial pulpits, their doctrine and style of ministry meeting with strong opposition from the ecclesiastical authorities. Some respectable individuals who had learned the value of the gospel and felt its

---

* Mr. Wesley's Journal abounds with interesting references to Dublin. Since his time Methodism has multiplied its chapels and its members in Dublin, and stimulated the Established Church and others to zealous efforts.—EDITOR.

power, opened a correspondence with Lady Huntingdon, known to the world as having consecrated her all to God her Saviour; and, in connection with her plans, the old meeting-house in Plunket street, then unoccupied, was engaged, and there the true doctrine of Christ was preached, and prayer and praise presented, in presence of crowded assemblies, often including persons of rank, by a variety of truly godly and able men—clergymen of the Establishment and dissenting ministers. Among them were the two just mentioned, and the Rev. Rowland Hill, of London, and the Rev. Samuel Pierce, of Birmingham. Much good was done by converting sinners and infusing spirit and energy among Protestants, in that house of worship. In 1783, the late well-known Bethesda chapel was built by William Smyth, Esq., for the purpose of providing the preaching of the gospel in connection with the forms of the Established Church. It has been well said, that at the time when religion was at a low ebb in the Church of Ireland, and evangelical men were made the objects of ridicule and reproach, the Bethesda chapel was a beacon of light in the midst of darkness.*

We will now present the reader with a general notice of the principal additions, combining architectural distinction with public utility, made to the city during the latter half of the eighteenth century. They were—1st. The Lying-in Hospital, in Great Britain street, fronting towards Sackville street. In 1745, Dr. Mosse, eminent

---

* See Memoirs of Robert and James Haldane.

equally in his profession and for his philanthropy, opened at his own expense a large house in George's street for the accommodation of poor lying-in women: this was the first institution of the kind in the empire, and from it sprang a corresponding one in London. In 1751, the first stone was laid of the spacious premises for its accommodation, an undertaking towards which the parliament liberally contributed. 2d. The truly beautiful frontage of Trinity College.* 3d. The Royal Exchange, on Cork hill, founded in 1769, and opened in ten years afterwards. Previously the general rendezvous for business among mercantile men had been a portion of the Tholsel. The present Exchange, though not one of the largest, is considered one of the most richly finished structures in the city. 4th. In 1773, the Blue Coat Hospital, for the education of the sons and grandsons of decayed citizens, was commenced on Oxmantown green. 5th. The present Custom House, which is considered the most sumptuous edifice of the kind in the world, was commenced in 1781, opened for despatch of business in 1791, and, with docks, quays, furniture, etc., including accommodation for the Irish department of excise, had cost the public, by the year

---

* John Wesley, in his Journal for April 6, 1758, says, "We walked round the college, and saw what was accounted most worthy of observation. The new front is exceeding grand; and the whole square (about as large as Peckwater in Christ Church) would be beautiful, were not the windows too small, as every one will see when the present fashion is out of date."—EDITOR.

1811, upwards of half a million of money. 6th. The Four Courts, comprising under one roof the several courts of Chancery, Queen's Bench, Common Pleas, and Exchequer. These courts were at first and for a long time ambulatory, being as often held at Carlow as in Dublin. In the beginning of the eighteenth century, they occupied a building in Christ Church lane, erected for the purpose in 1695, which also bore the name of the Four Courts. The foundation of the present edifice was laid by the Duke of Rutland, then lord lieutenant, with great ceremony in 1786, and it was subsequently completed, at a cost of about £200,000, in a style which well bespeaks the majesty of the law. It is said not to equal the design of the architect, through the impossibility of obtaining ground in the rear of the premises, sufficient to allow of the central portion being made to stand somewhat retired from the line of frontage shown by the two wings. 7th. Sir Patrick Dun's Hospital, the foundation of which was laid in 1800.

With the above enumeration we might include the present Essex bridge, built in 1755; Queen's bridge, 1768; and Carlisle bridge, opened in 1794; also the erection of Granite quays on both sides of the river for confining its waters, which previously flowed up to within eighty feet of the college, and occasioned alarming inundations upon that and the opposite bank. The grand canal was commenced in 1772, and the royal canal in 1789, the former entering the river below the city on the south side, and the latter on its opposite part on the north, both canals opening a communication from the river Shannon with the metropolis and the English channel. But the greatest undertaking of this period was the building of the Poolbeg lighthouse in Dublin Bay, commenced in 1764, with the wall, or pier, about three miles in length, connecting it with the city at Ringsend, and having the Pigeon-house Fort midway between the two. This lighthouse was the first which was provided with *candles*, as an improvement upon *coal-fires*. About the same time, candles were substituted for coal-fires in the Howth light; and in course of time the candles themselves had to give place to argand lamps with reflectors, much to the advantage of the mariner.

The silk manufacture of Dublin was, in 1764, placed by authority of parliament under the care of the Royal Dublin Society, through whose excellent arrangements the sales, at an establishment opened in the city, for disposing of silk goods, reached an average of £70,000 a year, and the silk manufacture itself, in Dublin, attained the highest state of prosperity. But, after a few years, the legislature forbade the society appropriating funds to support any house in which Irish silk goods were sold; and that prohibition seriously affected the manufacture.

About 1706, two persons established a cotton manufactory, and employed six hundred looms. Large sums, both individual capitals and even grants from parliament, were expended in promoting that branch of industry, yet with only limited success. The trade however held on, and until recently a respectable amount of business was done.

In the year 1782, persons chiefly connected with the university associated together for the purpose of investigating general literary and scientific subjects, and questions connected with the ancient history and circumstances of Ireland. In a few years, they obtained a charter of incorporation under the name of the "Royal Irish Academy," for the study of polite literature, science, and antiquities. Its "Transactions" present a collection of papers which do honor to the body from which they emanate, and its Museum abounds in articles interesting to the curious in what belongs to Erin's ancient times.

The name of "Dean Kirwan" is still mentioned in Dublin, though half a century has gone since his day, as that of a perfect master and model of pulpit eloquence, who thrilled, and almost did his will with the audiences he addressed. He had been a Roman Catholic, but conformed. It is reported that the late Mr. Grattan said before the House of Commons that, as occupied by Kirwan, "the preacher's desk became the throne of light." He confined himself to appeals for charity, and so great was his popularity that the military were in attendance to keep order and secure a passage to the church for the nobility and gentry, of whom the vast congregation on those occasions was almost entirely composed. His sermons were most carefully elaborated, and were spoken, not read. The collection upon one occasion amounted to *eight hundred pounds*. By his published discourses we are led to believe that his *forte* was *delivery*, including appropriate and correct intonation and action, rather than any thing extraordinary in the quality or quantity of thought conveyed. It cannot be said that he was what is called *evangelical*. But it is reported that before his death his mind underwent an important change, and that he spoke of his former preaching thus—" I can compare it to nothing better than to *Nero fiddling when Rome was on fire.*"

During the American war, when Ireland was in constant danger of invasion from the fleets of hostile continental powers hovering on her shores, she had not more than five thousand regular troops for her defence. The town of Belfast applied to the British government for increased protection. The reply was that all the aid available for the purpose, was half a troop of dismounted horse and half a company of invalids. The inhabitants met the exigency themselves, by forming a corps of volunteers. " The noble example was ardently followed by the country at large, and Ireland soon beheld starting up, with a scenic rapidity, a self-collected, self-disciplined body of forty thousand volunteers." In 1778, the first Dublin regiment was formed, under the command of the Duke of Leinster. The whole force reached the number of eighty thousand men. At their head was the Earl of Charlemont. The host included the wealth and intelligence, as it did the popular strength, of the country. The government supplied arms, and though the volunteers were not called into active service, they received the thanks of parliament for their loyalty, patriotism, and zeal. But the confederation considered itself formed for the good of the country, and therefore did not limit its views to repelling an invader. It aimed to obtain the redress of Ireland's wrongs. Delegates from its several portions met in Dublin in November, 1783. They marched in procession, with an imposing military display, to open their deliberations in the Rotunda, and continued their assembly for several weeks. By their spirited discussions and resolves, they obtained from the legislature, then sitting, (and of which body not a few of them were members,) several measures favorable to the trade and independence of the country. By degrees, however, fears arose in some quarters that the convention was going too far. The tide turned and ebbed. Yet numbers remained firm in purpose for achieving what they accounted the complete emancipation "of their own, their native land." They were encouraged by the recent example of the United States. The French Revolution gave increased power to their movements. The members of the body were for the most part Roman Catholics; but with them others sympathized in seeking the abolition of civil penalties for religious opinions. A degree of relief was granted to the Roman Catholics, in 1793. Three years more had not expired when societies of United Irishmen were formed in all parts of the country. Separation from England and the establishment of a Republican government was projected. Thousands upon thousands were being privately drilled and disciplined to the use of arms in the metropolis and elsewhere. It is said that their numbers amounted to half a million. The leaders, disappointed of aid from France, and perhaps finding discouragement, if not desertion, arising in the masses, thought it wise to delay the crisis no longer, and May the 23d, 1798, was fixed for a general insurrection.

Of this purpose the government were apprised some months before, and in March took their steps accordingly. Many persons were arrested: among others, Lord Edward Fitzgerald, who died of the wounds he received in the struggle at his capture. The city was placed under martial law. "Throughout the capital, against which the first fury of the insurgents was to be directed,'and where, from its extent, there could never be a certainty that the attack had not already begun, the consternation was universal. The spectacle of awful preparation, which promised security, gave no tranquillity. In the panic of the moment, the measures for security became so many images of danger. The military array and bustle in some streets—the silence and desertion of others—the names of the inhabitants registered on every door —the suspension of public amusements, and almost of private intercourse—the daily proclamations—prayers put up in the churches for the general safety—families flying to England—partings which might be final—every thing oppressed the imagination that a great public convulsion was at hand. The parliament and the courts of justice, with a laudable attention to the forms of the constitution, continued their sittings; but the strange aspect of senators and advocates transacting civil business in the garb of soldiers, reminded the spectator that the final dependence of the state was upon a power beyond the laws. In Dublin, the domestics of the principal citizens had disappeared, and gone off to join the insurgents; while those who could not be seduced to accompany them became the more suspected from this proof of their fidelity: they remained, it was apprehended, for the sole purpose of being spies upon their masters, and coöperators in their intended destruction; and thus, to the real dangers of a general design against the government, were added all the imaginary horrors of a project of individual vengeance."

The writer of the above, Mr. H. J. Curran, in the Life of his father, the celebrated John Philpot Curran, states further:—"Upon the appointed day, the explosion took place. The shock was dreadful. The imagination recoils from a detail of the scenes that followed." "After a short and sanguinary struggle, the insurgents were crushed. The numbers of them who perished in the field, or on the scaffold, or were exiled, are said to have amounted to fifty thousand: the losses upon the side of the Crown have been computed at twenty thousand lives.

Upon the rebellion of 1798 followed the Legislative Union between Great Britain and Ireland, a measure which encountered strenuous opposition in and beyond the parliament of the latter country, but was at length carried; and on the

27th of March, 1800, the Houses of Lords and Commons waited on the Viceroy at the Castle with the "Articles of Union." The bills passed in College Green and St. Stephen's for consummating it received the royal assent; and thus, in all due form, the two islands came to have thenceforth only one legislature, as they had for centuries been subject to one crown. May they, not merely linked together by law, but influenced by the fear of God and the faith of his gospel, strive in all integrity and good-will, with wisely directed and unceasing endeavor, to become, according to their respective capabilities, blessings to each other, and, as of one heart and of one soul, an agency for multiplying blessing to the world!

SECTION VII.

DUBLIN SINCE THE UNION WITH GREAT BRITAIN TO THE YEAR EIGHTEEN HUNDRED AND FIFTY.

On the 1st day of January, 1801, "The Imperial United Standard was first displayed upon Bedford Tower, Dublin Castle, in consequence of the Act of Legislative Union becoming an operative Law."

Widely contrasted were the feelings with which persons recognized the flag on that memorable morning, according as they were favorable or otherwise to the new relative position which it symbolized as existing between Ireland and Great Britain.

Great as may be the aggregate benefits of the "Union" to the two countries, it was unavoidable that Dublin itself should suffer by the abolition of the Irish parliament. The measure was to the metropolis what absenteeism is to the country. According to Dr. Walsh, Dublin, before the Union, was the constant or occasional residence of 249 temporal peers, 22 spiritual peers, and 300 members of the House of Commons. This unquestionably created and sustained for the city a large amount of business, which was the more important from the limited extent of Dublin's manufactures, mercantile transactions, and enterprise. Yet the city has not altogether sunk under the privation, as many of its inhabitants and others foreboded. Changes in the sources and modes of industry and acquisition may take place without absolute ruin to a community; and such changes must, in the progress of society, frequently occur. Dublin has survived, under the Union, for half a century; and it may be hoped that the century's end will see Ireland's metropolis far more flourishing and prosperous than when, at the century's beginning, the Union flag first floated on Bedford Tower.

The Irish parliament having ceased to exist, the stately structure built for its accommodation was no longer wanted. In the year 1783, a company had been formed by Act of Parliament and charter, called the "Bank of Ireland," and had hitherto occupied premises in Mary's Abbey. An Act was now passed in the Imperial Parliament, authorizing the sale of the edifice in College Green to the Bank of Ireland. Alterations were made in it to accommodate it to its new purpose, and others to render it more secure if not more beautiful. What had been the House of Commons, where Grattan, Plunket, Flood, Burke, Saurin, and other men of might, gave forth eloquent argument which might have honored the Pnyx of Athens or the senate-house of Rome, was changed into the bank cash-office; and the House of Lords, with its tapestried walls, where nobles assembled in deliberation upon their nation's interests, and where the representative of majesty sat on the vice-regal throne, was changed into a room for holding meetings of Bank proprietors.

The month of July, in 1803, was made memorable in Dublin by an insurrection headed by Robert Emmet, a man of ability and of a reputable position in society. On the evening of the 23d, the highly respected Lord Kilwarden, chief justice of the King's Bench, returning from the courts in his carriage, was attacked by an infuriate rabble and murdered on the spot. The outbreak " resembled a riot rather than an insurrection, and was alarming only because it was unexpected; for, notwithstanding the momentary panic which it excited, in a few hours the public tranquillity was restored."

For twenty years the peace of the city remained unbroken by any serious disturbance. In 1830, the government suppressed the Society of Friends of Ireland, the Anti-Union Society, and the Volunteers of Ireland, as endangering the public tranquillity. During the year following, the late Daniel O'Connell, Esq., M.P., and seven others, were arrested for holding political meetings, contrary to proclamation. On the 8th of October, 1843, a public meeting to be held at Clontarf, under Mr. O'Connell, for promoting the repeal of the Union, was prevented by proclamation; and on the 14th of the same month informations were lodged against that gentleman and his son, with two Roman Catholic clergymen, and five other leaders in the movement, for a misdemeanor.

Their trial, one of the most arduous and generally exciting to the public mind of the empire, though not the most important, which has occurred in the administration of national justice, commenced on the 15th of January : on the 12th of February a verdict of "guilty" was returned ; and the convicted were committed to prison on the 30th of May. An appeal was carried before the House of Lords, who reversed the decision of the court below. The sensation produced upon all parties and classes in the city, when the news of this arrived, was most profound. It is said to have taken the prisoners themselves and their most sanguine friends by surprise. Throughout the city, but especially on the way to the Richmond Bridewell, where they were confined, all was intensely earnest but noiseless stir. In a day or two afterwards, they left the prison, but no riot or even lesser breach of the peace occurred.

The year 1848 was marked by more threatening movements than had appeared since the rebellion fifty years before. On the 18th of July, Dublin was proclaimed under the Crime and Outrage Act; and on the 26th the Habeas Corpus Suspension Act arrived in the city. But the transportation of John Mitchell, under the Treason Felony Act, for fourteen years, the violent proceedings of other disaffected parties, with their arrest, conviction, and condemnation for high treason, and the commutation of their sentence of death to expatriation, are things fresh in general recollection.

Of calamitous events in Dublin since the

century began, several must not pass unadverted to. In the latter part of the summer of 1832, the Asiatic cholera appeared for the first time, and hurried off its thousands of victims. On the night of Sunday, January the 6th, 1839, a most terrific storm swept across the city. The evening was heavily still and warm; about ten o'clock, P.M., the wind had risen; by one next morning it was raging; from three to four was at its greatest fury; and it scarcely subsided till the Tuesday following. Just at the midnight of the Sunday, the Bethesda chapel and premises were on fire. The view of the city from the rear of houses on the canal bank, between Portobello and Charlemont street, was appallingly awful; the roar of the tempest, the trembling of those comparatively sheltered dwellings, the blaze in the distance lighting up the sky so as to render objects almost visible as at noon, the consciousness of the havoc which was being made, and, if possible, the yet far-greater havoc that was threatened by the flames, awoke sensations which approached what we might suppose would be produced by foretokens of the heavens passing away with a great noise, the elements melting with fervent heat, and the earth and all things therein being burned up. In April, 1849, the cholera again carried off numbers, continuing to prevail with intermitting violence till October. On the 18th of April, 1850, between three and four in the afternoon, a storm like a tornado suddenly burst upon the city, accompanied with thunder, lightning, and a torrent of hail-stones, many of them nearly the size of walnuts, by which property to the value of £27,000 was destroyed.

Under the head of joyous occurrences in the course of this period the loyal Irish rank as chief far above all others, the visits of two of their sovereigns. His majesty, King George IV., landed at Howth on the 12th of August, 1821, and came in state to the city on the 17th, amidst the warmest acclamations of his subjects. On two nights the city was illuminated. His majesty visited the public institutions, presided at the installation of the Knights of St. Patrick in St. Patrick's Cathedral, and finally embarked at Dunleary, thenceforth "Kingstown," on the 3d of September. The king left behind him favorable impressions of his respect for the religious convictions and feelings of others. It is said that having proposed to visit a nobleman residing a few miles from the city on a Sunday, it was intimated to him by his lordship that the arrangement might occasion much disregard of the Sabbath in the neighborhood, when his majesty promptly changed the appointment to the next day, Monday. It has also been stated, that when he went in state to a ball given by the Knights of St. Patrick in the Rotunda, all the knights being, as a matter of duty to their sovereign, present at the entrance to receive him; the king recognising one member of the illustrious order in attendance whom he knew to be otherwise minded than to be at home in such engagements, took him most cordially by the hand and said,

"Ah! —— you're here: well, I know you don't like these sorts of things: good-night, good-night!" so graciously giving him liberty to retire, and then passed on.

The evening of the 5th of August, 1849, saw anchoring at Kingstown harbor a royal squadron of ten men-of-war, with the Victoria and Albert yacht, having on board her majesty Queen Victoria, with the prince consort, and others of the royal family. On the following morning, the queen, accompanied by Prince Albert and the royal children, made their public entry into Dublin, where preparations on the most extensive and magnificent scale had been made to give her majesty the best possible welcome to her Irish metropolis. Nothing could exceed the enthusiasm with which she was everywhere by all parties and classes greeted, in her progress through the city to the Viceregal Lodge in the Park. At night, the illuminations were most brilliant, and, in many instances, on the costliest scale, but the throngs out to witness them were subjected to the heaviest fall of rain that had occurred for many years. Her majesty during her short stay visited the Glasnevin Gardens, and some of the leading public establishments. An American republican can hardly suppress a smile while reading the following: "When inspecting the fine library of the College, a copy of Sallust of the fifteenth century, having in it the autograph of Mary Queen of Scots, was shown to her majesty, who was pleased to favor the university with another autograph still more interesting and estimable, by writing her name on a blank leaf of the Book of Kells, immediately beneath which Prince Albert also affixed his signature, each bearing the date of the day which marked this incident." A levee and drawing-room were held; by far the most numerous and splendid ever seen in Dublin; and the uniformly condescending and gracious manner of the queen on all occasions won for her all hearts. The elegant neatness and simplicity of her majesty's dress particularly struck the common people. After partaking of a collation with the Duke and Duchess of Leinster, at Carston, on the morning of the 10th, her majesty and the Prince Albert, with the royal children and attendants, went by rail to Kingstown, and there embarked. The scene on that occasion baffles our attempt adequately to describe it. The day was delightfully fine. The myriads of human beings crowding every spot where standing could be had on land or water; the men-of-war, with other sailing and steam vessels, including many belonging to the yacht clubs, besides boats almost beyond count, having every shred of color hoisted and every yard manned; the roar of cannon saluting from the quay and ships, as her majesty set foot on board, amidst yet mightier thunderings from the densely thronging masses of loyal hearts, whose acclamations almost drowned the roar of the artillery; the royal squadron moving out to sea, the ship La Hogue, of 60 guns, having taken the lead, firing her salute, with her flags all hoisted, and her yards covered with her crew; above all, the gliding, in truly royal style, of the Victoria and Albert close in along the pier with its multitudes, her majesty on deck ordering the royal standard to be lowered and raised again (an honor never done before except for a royal personage) in token of her gracious farewell to her Dublin subjects—formed altogether a spectacle the like of which no party present had ever seen before, and which all judged it next to impossible they should ever see again.

The most prominent public edifices erected in Dublin since the Union, have been :—1st. The King's Inns, commenced and opened before, but the greater portion of it built in 1802. 2d. St. George's Church, begun in the same year. 3d. The College of Surgeons in Stephen's green, founded in 1806. 4th. The Castle Chapel, a gem of architecture, and a cabinet of carved work, begun in 1807, and opened in 1814, 5th. Nelson's Monument, in 1808. 6th. The General Post Office (far excelling for its size, its junior in St. Martin's-le-Grand,) founded in 1814, and completed four years afterwards. The National Bank, founded 1842 ; with the termini of the South-Western, Midland, and Drogheda Railways, in the past four years.

The literary and scientific, educational, medical, surgical, commercial, benevolent, and religious associations and institutions, to which the past fifty years have given birth in Dublin are so numerous, that it would be difficult to make a selection for the purpose of explaining their nature and objects in these pages.

Notice was taken in the last section of a reviving attention to evangelical truth in Dublin, particularly in the Plunket street and Bethesda chapels. Persons belonging to these places of worship, with others of the Mary's Abbey and Bishop street congregations, formed themselves into a society for bringing over ministers of the gospel from London and other places, to supply, by their visits for a few weeks, the lack of Christian teaching in the city. Since this century began, evangelical piety has greatly increased. Within the last twenty-five years particularly has this happy change been manifest in the Established Church; evangelical activity prevails in many of its parish churches, ecclesiastical activity in all; and to these have been added several voluntary chapels in which justification by faith is constantly held forth as the only doctrine on which man can safely rest his hope before God, and which is to be the guide of his life and the joy of his heart while journeying to immortality. It is no unreasonable digression from our narrative, we trust, to pause and affectionately inquire of our reader whether he has experimentally known this great truth? Whether he has ever felt in all its importance the reality of eternal things? his state by nature as a perishing sinner? the necessity for repentance from dead works, of a living faith in Christ, and of the regenerative influence of the Holy Spirit? Fifty or sixty years ago, the Sacred Scriptures were generally uncared for; there were then only two booksellers in Dublin who sold pocket Bibles:

one of them had but *two* new ones, and the other had not one *new* one, though he had some two or three *old* ones. Now, in profession at least, "The Bible, and the Bible only, is the religion of Protestants." At the beginning of this century, family worship was a rarity among Protestant households: now it is observed by a considerable proportion of them. Then, there were two or three Sunday schools: now, it would be difficult to mention a part of the city which is not supplied with them. Then, the theatre was well sustained: now the reverse is the case. Then, except the Methodists, scarcely a preacher in the city opened his lips to warn Romanists against their delusions and teach them the gospel: now, by many ministers in and out of the establishment, witness is constantly being borne for the doctrine of Christ in opposition to the spirit of antichrist, and large classes meet for discussing the points at issue between the two. Then, practical godliness was as contemned, as it was rare among Protestants: now, perhaps, the danger is of its being assumed and professed where it does not exist, through its having become to a certain extent frequent and respected.

On the whole, there is probably no city in the world where so great an alteration for the better has taken place in the state and habits of a Protestant population as in Dublin. But the people must press on.

This revival of sound piety among the Protestants has been accompanied by, if it have not provoked to, greatly increased vigilance and energetic working among the Roman Catholics of the community, who by their many new chapels and other edifices, their thronged attendance at their places of worship, their large pecuniary contributions towards objects specially their own, and their clerical and lay activities for their church, might well put to the blush persons who are yet slumbering in Protestant denominations.

The following general statement of the population at different periods during the last and present centuries, will enable the reader to judge of its progress :

In 1728—146,075.	In 1821—185,881.
1753—128,570.	1831—203,650.
1777—138,208.	1834—240,273.
1798—182,370.	1841—232,726.
1812—176,610.	1851—254,850.

Showing an increase in Dublin of 22,124 persons between 1841 and 1851.

The woollen, linen, cotton, and silk manufactures of Dublin are described as well nigh extinct, notwithstanding several efforts to revive them. "Brewing, iron-casting, and cabinet-making are the principal manufactures in a thriving state." The number of vessels entered with cargoes from foreign parts was, in 1840, 247, and in 1850, 462. "Very laudable exertions are making to establish a respectable foreign import trade; and from the business habits of the people, there is every reason to anticipate a result beneficial to the spirited undertakers. Several cargoes of tea from China have been imported, and also importations from Calcutta and the Mauritius. The importations from the West Indies have also increased, The best symptoms of the improvement of the trade of this port, is found in the annual amount of custom's duties on articles of home consumption. From 1821 to 1832, the receipts were nearly stationary at about £600,000. In 1850, they had increased to £874,943."

We have seen that in the former half of the last century, Dublin had three newspapers: it has now twenty-eight, of which three are daily, sixteen weekly, five thrice a week, two twice a week, and two monthly. It has also several periodicals, among which are the Dublin University Magazine, the Dublin Review, a leading Roman Catholic journal; and the Irish Quarterly Review, lately commenced.

A division is made of the city into two nearly equal parts by the river Liffey, over which there are nine bridges, two of them of iron, and the extent of quays along its banks is two miles and a half. It would be impossible to compress into a small portion of our historical sketch of the city any thing like a detail of the various "lions" of the place: for those particulars, recourse must be had to the guide-books, with one out of the many of which no visitor should omit to supply himself. The greatest objects of interest are the University, with its Library of 120,000 volumes, its Museum, and various other buildings—the Royal Dublin Society House, including the Library, Museums, and Schools, together with its Garden at Glasnevin—the Museum of the Royal Irish Academy—the Bank of Ireland, especially its Printing-Office with its mechanism, the precursor and type of that in the Bank of England. If possible, too, the visitor should obtain a view of the Bank, with the College on his right hand, King William's statue on his left, and Westmoreland street towards the river—as seen from the bottom of Grafton street, on a clear night with the moon at full. The Castle, particularly its chapel, the Four Courts, Post-Office, with Sackville street, the Exchange, the Custom-House, must not be passed over; while there are various other edifices upon or within which a visitor may look with pleasure, or with profit, as the case may be.

Dublin has a position above any other city in the United Kingdom, except London, which is the seat of the British court, in being the residence of a viceroy. The abolition of this office was mooted some time ago, but it seems now agreed that matters shall for the present remain *in statu quo*. The "Castle," however, is certainly not what it ought to be as a viceregal palace, especially compared with the public buildings of the city.

There are in the city two cathedrals, twenty parochial churches, and about the same number of subsidiary chapels, belonging to the Established Church. The Methodists have eight chapels; the Presbyterians, five; the Independents, three; the Society of Friends, two; the

Unitarians, two; the Baptists, Moravians, Welsh Methodists, Christian Brethren, Jews, and one or two other bodies, one each. The Roman Catholics have nine parochial churches, six belonging to different orders of friars, one Jesuit church, three monasteries, and eight convents. Twenty-two hospitals or infirmaries, with a variety of dispensaries, administer medical or surgical relief, general or specific, to the Dublin poor. The city has two institutions for the deaf and dumb; two for the blind; four penitentiaries; several education boards, of which the principal are the Government Commissioners, the Church Education Society, and the Sunday-School Society of Ireland; three Ragged Schools; the Hibernian Bible Society, and some others, for circulating the Scriptures, with about a dozen institutions for directing or otherwise aiding the propagation of the gospel at home or abroad; several Protestant Orphan Societies, asylums for the aged and infirm, and numerous other benevolent agencies on a more or less extensive scale.

How much the city has extended as time has rolled, may be understood by comparing its present range with the accounts given in former sections of its population, streets, etc. Within the last two centuries there has been added to it by far the greater portion of the liberty, and nearly all the streetage, etc., lying to the west of the Castle and on the north side of the Liffey. The increase includes Mountjoy square, Rutland square, Merrion square, Fitzwilliam square, and Stephen's green: the last named is not the latest formed, but we introduce it last for the sake of stating that it is the largest square in Europe, being nearly a mile in circumference.

The city of Dublin is under the jurisdiction of a lord mayor, whose official residence, the Mansion House, is in Dawson street. The corporation consists of the lord mayor, fifteen aldermen, and forty-five town councillors, elected yearly in the proportion of one alderman and three councillors from each of the fifteen municipal wards into which the city is divided. The police force of the city and suburbs is upwards of 1000 strong, arranged under seven divisions. The military amount to about 6000, whose principal barracks are the Portobello, Richmond, Royal, Ship street, Mountjoy, Island Bridge, Aldborough House, Beggar's Bush, and the Pigeon House Fort.

West of the city is the Phœnix Park, the word *Phœnix* being a corruption of the Irish *Fionnuisge*, pronounced short *Finniské*, and signifying fair or clear water, the name given to the ancient manor from a spring in a glen not far from the entrance to the Lodge, and long known, celebrated, and much resorted to as a chalybeate spa. The formation of the park began in 1662, by the Duke of Ormond, then lord-lieutenant, through the appropriation of the above manor, (which had reverted to the crown after belonging to the Knights Templars at Kilmainham,) as a royal deer-park, and the purchase of some adjoining lands to render it of the desired size. Other additions have been made since, and its contents are now nearly two thousand acres. In the Park are the Viceregal Lodge, the country residence of the Viceroy, a simple, unimposing structure, with one hundred and sixty acres in demesne and gardens; lodges for the chief and under-secretaries; the Hibernian School for Soldiers' Children; the Military Infirmary; the Constabulary Barracks; Military Magazine; the Ordnance Survey Dépôt, and some other buildings, together with the Wellington Testimonial, the Phœnix Column, and the Zoological Gardens. One thousand three hundred acres of the park are free to the public.

The suburbs on the south side of the city are extending fast. The township of Rathmines is the most frequented, and considered to be the most salubrious portion of the environs. The Dublin mountains form a fine background to it as approached from the city.

To the south-east of the city, at a distance of about seven miles, is Kingstown and its Royal Harbor, to which vessels have access at all times of the tide, and which is the port for the mail packets and government vessels. The Dublin and Kingstown Railway affords a quick transit between the two places. From the top of Killiney Hill commanding views are obtained of the range terminating with Dublin to the north, the Dublin mountains on the west, those of Wicklow and Bray Head on the south, and the English Channel on the east.

Many paragraphs might be taken up with allusions to places and objects, interesting from their antiquity or otherwise, which stud the country around Ireland's metropolis. But we have not room to introduce them.

And now, with warm assurances of our good wishes, do we bid Dublin, for the present, adieu! Our heart was with her ere we undertook to sketch her progress from infancy to her present matured and established growth; and as we proceeded, the more kindly and strongly did our sympathies cluster around her. She has had her many times of distress and peril. Her times of prosperity have been hitherto few. But dawn, now brightening, promises her a glorious sunrise. Much, as to its being "a morning without clouds" ushering in a day of blessing, depends on her moral and religious course. The righteousness that exalts a nation is the true elevation of a city.

THE END.

www.ingramcontent.com/pod-product-compliance
Lightning Source LLC
Chambersburg PA
CBHW031440160426
43195CB00010BB/796